FEAR IS NOT AN OPTION

FEAR

IS NOT

AN

OPTION

MONICA BERG

Kabbalah Centre Publishing is a registered DBA of
Kabbalah Centre International, Inc.

For further information:

The Kabbalah Centre
1062 S. Robertson Blvd., Los Angeles, CA 90035
155 E. 48th St., New York, NY 10017

1.800.Kabbalah www.kabbalah.com

Printed in USA, November 2017

ISBN: 978-1-57189-964-4

TABLE OF CONTENTS

Foreword 9

Introduction 10

Part 1: The Anatomy Of Fear
Healthy Fear 17
Real Fear 27
Illogical Fear 31
Get to Know Your Fear 37

Part 2: My Journey Through Fear
Schizophrenia – It's Not Contagious 45
Anorexia – I Don't Have to Eat 51
David – I'm Still Not in Control 61
Josh – My Body Has Betrayed Me 65
Miriam – True Surrender 75
Abigail – Becoming a Channel 87
Fear Is Not an Option 95

Part 3: How You Can Live Fearlessly
Consciousness for Living Fearlessly 101
Fixed vs. Growth Mindset 102
You're Not Unlucky, You're Fearful 103
The Power of Perspective 105
Mind, Body, & Spirit:
Applying a Shifted Perspective 106
Fear of the Unknown 111
Shame of Wanting 113

Fear of Failure & Rejection 117
Fear & Letting Go 122
Fear & Relationships 123

Seven Tools for Working Through Your Fears 129
Tool 1: Naming Your Fears 130
Tool 2: Burning Your Fears 132
Tool 3: Diminishing Your Fears 133
Tool 4: Trim Tabs 136
Tool 5: Make Your Anti-Fear Mantra 138
Tool 6: Engage Your Body 140
Tool 7: Time Travel 141

Make an Action Plan 145
Step 1: Plan for the Morning 146
Step 2: Challenge Fear-Based Thoughts 147
Step 3: Exposure 150
Step 4: Create Your Exposure Hill 154

Seven Things I Want My Daughters to Know to
Become Fearless Women 159

Epilogue 165

Acknowledgments 167

References 174

Foreword

I am the voice in your head that says
you aren't **GOOD ENOUGH,** not **STRONG
ENOUGH**, not **SMART ENOUGH.**
I am the one who keeps you SMALL.
Who **STILLS** your tongue,
who **QUIETS** your passionate voice.
I am the one who **STOPS** you.
Who says **NO**, who tells you to **EXPECT LESS**
because that's what you deserve.
I make your hands **TREMBLE**, your heart **RACE**,
and your palms **SWEAT.**
I keep you up at night and give power to your
DOUBTS.

My name is **FEAR.**

Introduction

Kabbalah teaches that we have come into this world to grow spiritually and to make a positive impact on the world. Our inherent nature is at odds with growth as we tend to want to stay in our comfort zone, but that is not the realm in which we ultimately want to live. In order to transform ourselves and reach our greatest potential, we need to embrace discomfort. If we seek comfort first, we miss the purpose for which we came into this world. Through the application and embodiment of the wisdom of Kabbalah, we come to understand that challenges are opportunities for growth. Often we are faced with these challenges in pursuit of our most passionate goals, but it is through life's challenges that we can find the greatest gifts.

What gets in the way of achieving our goals? FEAR.

While fear was designed to be an effective warning system, it can very easily become something we unconsciously use as a guide. The kabbalist, the Baal Shem Tov, teaches that fear takes small, insignificant things and makes them huge. Imagine you are standing outside, and you are surrounded by natural wonder. The trees are auburn, the sun is warm on your skin, and the sky has a pink hue. A babbling stream trickles through a meadow just ahead of you and you hear birds chirping and the gentle rustle of leaves in the breeze. You are in a place of endless beauty that brings you serenity, peace, and calm.

Now imagine if you took something as insignificant as two pennies and used them to cover your eyes. Suddenly the beauty, peace, and tranquility you just experienced has been replaced by darkness.

You took an action that obscured your ability to see, and unknowingly, this is something we do often. We shift our focus to small insignificant things and make them very important, allowing them to "cover our eyes" and take reign over our lives. We create "pennies" with our stress, anxiety, problems, and fear, blocking out all the beauty that exists around us. When fears arise they act just like those pennies, and we are no longer able to see everything that is available to us.

A few years ago, I was in London to give a talk about living fearlessly. I felt pressure because my talk was due to begin in fifteen minutes and my Uber driver was hopelessly lost. He was armed with a GPS and false confidence in his navigation abilities. I kept calm and understood that he didn't know how to swim and had fallen into the deep end. When we passed the US Embassy, I realized just how far away we were. I knew, given where I needed to be, that if I was going to make my seminar, I was going to have to sprint, in my heels and in light rain, to get there hopefully no more than five minutes late. I politely directed him to the nearest recognizable street, hopped out, and ran as quickly as I could to my destination.

The irony isn't lost on me – I was afraid of being late to a seminar on living fearlessly. One at which I was speaking, no less. However, it is spot on as to what I hope this book will illuminate. As my palms started to perspire on this endless drive, I stopped listening to the voice of fear in my head and instead directed my attention to the radio, on which a woman was speaking about a book she had written on fear. I may have been late, but as a result I was given greater clarity about what I was hoping to relate in all things regarding fear.

The woman was explaining how people can cope with their fears and learn to live with them. As she was speaking, I thought, I disagree. I take a completely different approach from hers. We don't want to cope with our fears or tolerate them – we want to eliminate them. Hearing the questions and comments that came in from the radio show listeners, I felt an even stronger desire to write this book.

The goal is to eradicate fear completely. But as we work toward this goal, we can come to an understanding that fear will still arise. I began studying Kabbalah at age 17, just before all of my major life challenges. Unbeknownst to me at the time, I was being given tools with which to navigate what was ahead. Through sharing my experience of fear and the tools I used to remove it from my life, I hope to encourage and inspire readers to do the same by actively engaging with the process of eliminating fear and consistently making small changes toward progress.

Many people are living in a self-made prison of their own fears. A tolerable prison, one they can cope with, yet is still limiting.

I want you to be free from this self-made prison. I want you to be free of fear. And you can be.

PART 1:

The Anatomy of Fear

CHAPTER 1:

Healthy Fear

"Fear builds walls to bar the Light."

– Baal Shem Tov

We know a few things about fear. Namely, we know what it feels like and we know what we are afraid of, but what is fear? First let's understand the fundamentals of fear on a biological level.

Fear is an emotion caused by a perceived danger or threat that causes a change in our metabolic and organ functions and ultimately a change in our behavior, such as fleeing, hiding, or freezing.

Our fears may arise in response to something specific occurring in the present, or in anticipation of a future threat. This perception of danger can lead to confrontation with, or escape from the threat. In extreme cases, there can be an added paralysis. This is what we know as the "fight-or-flight" response. Our body's physical reaction to fear is almost entirely autonomic. We don't consciously trigger it or even know what's going on until it has run its course.

Fear manifests physically in our bodies due in large part to the amygdala - the part of your brain that releases a cascade of neurotransmitters that trigger the fight-or-flight response. The amygdala is the body's alarm system. It is responsible for the adrenaline rush that can save your life in an emergency. These symptoms can present themselves in a variety of ways, such as increased heart rate, shortness of breath, dizziness, nausea, digestive dysfunction, perspiration, shaking, and fainting.

Fear arises both through instinct and cognition. In other words, we are conditioned to many of our fears. This book focuses primarily on those fears that are not helpful, not serving to protect you from real danger, or are not contributing to your life.

Understanding that some fears are helpful and some are not is the foundation for beginning your journey of eliminating fears from your own life.

In the following pages, we will take a look at the different types of fears, which category they fall into, and how they impact your life both positively and negatively. I'd like to begin with healthy fears.

Do you enjoy scary movies? Do you get excited about rollercoasters? Are haunted houses something you gleefully frequent during Halloween?

All of these things are fun for most people. So much so that entire theme parks, experiences, and worldwide fan bases are dedicated to them. Healthy fear helps us discern safe situations from dangerous ones. We find fun in creating safe environments where we can experience healthy fear.

Healthy fear is a gift given to each and every one of us and typically manifests as a visceral, instinctual response to a physical threat. We need this type of fear for our survival and protection.

For example, if you are standing on a high ledge, healthy fear kicks in and cautions you to step back. It keeps you from falling off the cliff in the same way it keeps you from placing your hand too close to a flame. Think back to a time that your healthy fear response kicked in? What were the circumstances? What happened as a result? Healthy fear is our own built-in security guard, but its duality is evident and also curious. If this fear keeps us safe, why do we purposefully put ourselves in situations that trigger its responses?

This goes back to the physical response, adrenaline raises your heart rate and blood pressure, giving you a boost of energy, which is also what makes scaring yourself so much fun. Think of it in terms of learning how to ride a bike. At first you're scared. "What if I fall?" Then as you begin to learn, as your mind and body begin to work together to move the pedals and steer the wheels, that fear gives way to excitement. Before you know it, you're doing it.

Healthy fear keeps us safe and we should respect that instinct. However, we don't always listen to our healthy fears, as demonstrated in 1968 by social pyschologists Bibb Latané and John M. Darley with their Smoke Filled Room Test. Study participants are asked to sit in a room and fill out a questionnaire. One group of participants was put in the room alone, and the other group was in a room with two other people who were actually working for the researchers and were not participants in the study. A few minutes into each test, smoke is funneled into the room. Almost always, the participants who are alone in the room abandon their questionnaires and move to report the smoke immediately.

However, the participants in the room with others take exponentially longer to report the smoke, if they report it at all, even when smoke continues to fill the room to the point where they can barely see. This has come to be known as the Audience Inhibition Effect – the idea that people won't respond to an emergency situation out of fear of overreacting and embarrassment.[1]

Fear of embarrassing ourselves as a result of acting on our healthy fear causes danger to ourselves and others. Healthy fear responses should always be acknowledged. We want to dispel and completely erase fear from our lives with this one important exception.

We are armed with powerful intuitive responses to fear and those should ALWAYS be heeded.

Intuition is what we know without knowing why – those things in life we intuit without knowing why we know them. The Latin root of the word intuition, *tuere,* means "to guard, to protect." Our intuition is in place for precisely this reason. Just because we may not recognize the source of our intuition doesn't mean it isn't absolutely accurate. Most of us have experienced intuition as a certainty about things, like perhaps immediately trusting someone you just met or disliking someone you just met. Intuition shows up in our lives in so many ways; knowing that a flight you are on is going to be delayed, making other plans before your previous plans fall through, picking up and moving to a new city because it's just where you are supposed to be, or even buying a piece of furniture you know will be perfect in a house in which you don't yet live.

Intuition asserts itself abruptly and with obscure origins. Largely dismissed as fantasy or magic, intuition is, at least partially, a cognitive process. When we receive information from our environment, such as the tone of a voice, a facial expression, hand gesture, or body posture, our brain begins rapidly matching that input to stored memories. Our brains are wondrous and complex and capable of so much processing that happens beneath our consciousness. You may not know it, but the alarm bells that were set off by the expression on a coworker's face could have come from a mental matching to an expression that your hypercritical third grade teacher used to make.

Think about romantic chemistry. Often two people meet, have a wonderful conversation, and genuinely like and respect each other. However, that relationship will go nowhere if their pheromones are not attractive to the other person.

What does a pheromone smell like? We don't know, but our body certainly knows, and more than that, discerns what would make a good mate based upon the genetic differences relayed through those pheromones.

Often intuition is accompanied by an emotion, maybe evoking feelings of familiarity or even dread. Many of us have experienced a feeling, dream, or vision, either positive or negative, about something in our own lives or about those closest to us. We ignore these signals at our own peril. Women in particular will discredit their intuitive alarm bells about a person in order to avoid conflict or seem rude.

In Murray, Utah, 18-year old Carol DaRonch was approached by a man claiming to be a Murray Police Officer. He told her that someone had attempted to break into her car and then asked her to drive to the police station with him to file a report. As they were driving, Carol pointed out that they were on the wrong road, one that didn't lead to the station. When Carol questioned him further, the officer pulled over and tried to handcuff her. In the ensuing struggle she escaped. Later it was discovered that the "officer" was actually serial killer Ted Bundy. Carol was one of the few known to have escaped him unharmed.[2] By listening to her intuition and questioning the route he was taking, Carol saved her own life. This story is terrifying, but drives home how your intuition can literally save your life.

My advice, listen to your intuition and listen to your inner voice, your "gut." In the face of your intuition telling you something is off, don't try to reason with yourself, just listen to what your instincts are trying to tell you and take steps to ensure your safety. If you feel you should avoid a certain road, or the person standing in the elevator you are about to enter makes you feel uncomfortable, honor your intuition. The smoke filled room participants shut down their response to their healthy fear for a number of "rational" reasons. In the face of logic or appearing rude versus listening to your intuition, you should side with your intuition every time.

This book is about eliminating fear, however this type, healthy fear, is not a fear to eliminate because it exists to keep us safe.

CHAPTER 2:

Real Fear

R eal fear is very much based in reality. It is not the same as healthy fear, in the sense that it's not based on physical danger. We all experience the real fears of losing the people we love most, never achieving our dreams and aspirations, even the fear of our own death. Real fear is the truth that life is a terminal condition and it's based on something that is irrefutably real: Everything we do and everything we are has an expiration date. These manifestations of real fear are not physical, but rather existential. They are just as valid, because they are associated with real events like death, change, and pain.

The question then becomes, can these fears also consume us and keep us from living our life fully? Ultimately, yes. But, luckily, the choice is yours, because real fear can motivate us toward living our best life.

Real fears can be empowering. For instance, if you fear losing people you love, put your energy toward being completely engaged when spending time with them and fully appreciate that they are here now. Some fear growing old and the process of aging; perhaps this energy could be spent exercising and making dietary changes to ensure that the golden years are more healthful. Real fear can be used as a powerful motivation for using our thoughts and spending our time wisely. Real fear cannot be eliminated because it is legitimate, but it is in our control to transform it into something that is empowering instead of debilitating.

CHAPTER 3:

Illogical Fear

Illogical fear resides on the opposite end of the spectrum from real fear. It might feel the same, but it is typically triggered as a result of something hypothetical or altogether nonexistent. This in no way discounts or invalidates illogical fear as it can be greatly detrimental to your life. It keeps you worried, frantic, and insecure. It can hinder your life in a variety of ways and can lead to emotional distress, anxiety disorders, and physical manifestations. For example, people who experience extreme fright can develop painful migraines just hours later as a result of being startled. Unlike healthy fear, illogical fear should be released.

We are all balanced between two powerful forces-the positive and the negative. Kabbalah teaches that the positive draws us toward transformation. The negative feeds our ego and fulfills our desire for instant gratification. Both of these forces are significant for our spiritual development. While the benefits of the positive force are self-evident, the negative force gives us the opportunity to choose the direction of our lives. The positive force is our inherent perfection, and the negative side presents the challenges that help us to bring our perfection into the world. In order for there to be a positive side, a negative side must also exist. Without this duality, we would have no way to experience growth or realize our potential. However, many of us can become too mired, too associated with, too stuck in the negative side, thus hindering our fullest experience of life.

From this kabbalistic perspective, illogical fear comes from the negative side to make us upset, depressed, and to create obstacles on our path.

Whether big or small, this fear manifests for all of us in different ways. Spiders. Heights. Cockroaches. Flying. Is there a fear in your life that falls into this category? Perhaps it's driving on freeways? Claustrophobia? Public speaking? Imagine what your life would be like if this fear was eliminated.

For me, illogical fear manifested as a fear of elevators. This fear had been with me for as long as I can remember, since I was three or four. I would panic anytime I was in an elevator. This fear was so irrational and started at such an early age that it made me wonder if it was the residue from an early life experience that I couldn't recall. When my mother assured me that she never locked me in a cage or a closet, I then pondered if it was something I was bringing into this life from a past life experience.

When I moved to New York, my illogical fear began to set in again in a very real way. It is almost impossible to navigate New York City without getting on an elevator nearly every day. I love exercise, but I don't love traversing twenty flights of stairs on a daily basis. Which I have because of this illogical fear. On more than one occasion I've climbed twenty-seven flights of stairs to avoid taking an elevator. My fear was so elaborate that if I had just come back from a run and didn't have water, the idea of getting stuck in an elevator while feeling parched and dehydrated would send my mind spinning and my heart racing. However, I wanted to move to New York and decided this fear wasn't going to tag along. Though I didn't know how this fear developed, I came to terms with never discovering the root and decided it wasn't going to be a part of my future.

And that was that. Once you decide, you can change any reality. It takes commitment and mental work, but it absolutely can be done. I also used practical tools for overcoming illogical fears, which I will share later on in this book.

It sounds simple, but that is the thing about these silly fears. The only thing providing them sustenance is you. You feed the fear every time you give into it. You feed it, it becomes stronger, and its appetite grows. Once you make the decision to give fear the boot, it no longer has a place in your mind, and therefore, no place in your life. In the absence of the fear, your life will begin to unfold in incredible ways.

CHAPTER 4:

Get To Know Your Fear

"Of all the fears that bedevil
mankind, none is so terrifying as
fear of the unknown; what is
unknown can neither be avoided
nor controlled. By naming the
creatures of a newly formed world,
Adam became the master of his
environment."

-Rav Berg[3]

The "creatures" in the above quote are our
fears. The first step toward fearless living is

to identify your fears and "name" them. You can write them down here, or on a separate piece of paper.

It's not enough to simply think about them, you need to write them down, as the act of writing will make them more concrete. When you shed light on your fears, you release them. Below, write down any fears that arise when you think of these areas:

What are your fears in relationships?

1. _____

2. _____

3. _____

What are your fears in your career?

1. _____

2. _____

3. _____

What are your fears about your future?

1. _____

2. _____

3. _____

What do you worry about when you lie in bed at night?

1. _____

2. _____

3. _____

From these answers, identify your three biggest fears and write them below.

1. _____

2. _____

3. _____

Of these fears, can you identify which fears are healthy, illogical, or real?

_____

_____

_____

_____

_____

_____

PART 2:

My Journey Through Fear

CHAPTER 5:

Schizophrenia –
It's Not Contagious

I can recall my very first experience of feeling consumed by fear. When I was eight years old my family moved from Louisiana to California – Beverly Hills to be exact. Up until this move I had lived a quintessentially idyllic childhood. I was the happy child of a family of all daughters and my existence was, in many ways, sheltered. I hadn't experienced any violence, hadn't been privy to death or sickness, there was no trauma or stress.

My childhood was so pristine that I have specific memories as early as three-years-old of being joyful, carefree, and safe.

That all changed one afternoon at my grandparents' home, shortly after the move. Recalling this memory even now gives me pause. We were all gathered on a bright summer day for a family lunch. I had known my grandparents and had always enjoyed their visits to New Orleans. We now began spending nearly all downtime with aunts, uncles, and cousins – making up for lost time.

The move had its challenges, as all moves do, and I felt somewhat lonely, missing my friends and the safety of the life and routines I had loved. To make matters worse, my parents had lost all of their wealth. In a nutshell, the move to Los Angeles felt like an entry into the world of the unknown – the source of all my fears, as I came to understand.

As I was sitting at this luncheon, with all adults, more as an observer than a participant, the energy became tense and uncomfortable and even I, at age eight, could tell my parents' laughter had become forced. I had been playing at the table next to my mother and I looked up to see her older brother standing in the doorway. Something about him struck me as odd. His behavior was off somehow. Erratic. The conversation around the table started to taper off and then out of nowhere, there was a searing scream. I jumped.

My uncle was fueled with an intention that even he didn't understand and it was clear to me that he didn't have control of his actions. His behavior was terrifying, and somewhat violent. The adults instantly rose, though none of them seemed to know quite how to handle him. I wanted to hide and prayed my mother would grab my hand and whisk me out of the room. I didn't want to move out of fear I would call attention to myself – his attention. I was like a kid in a classroom trying to be still so the teacher wouldn't notice me and call me to the chalkboard. The last thing I wanted was to provoke him in any way.

He then pulled his pants down and exposed himself to everyone, screaming, shouting, and cursing at my grandparents. I was terrified. Finally, I felt a hand over my eyes and then I could pretend I wasn't there anymore.

A year later, I walked through my grandparents' home looking at old photographs of my mom and her siblings. I saw my grandparents in their younger days, my own mother at my age, and the happiness on everyone's faces. Then, I was struck by the image of a beautiful boy. He looked happy and confident. I didn't recognize him. I asked my mother who the striking, young boy was and was shocked to learn it was my uncle. She told me all about him. He had once been handsome and very self-assured. He had been admired during his teen years, had joined the army and had been engaged. He had been not only totally normal, but promising with a bright future. How could somone become the man I saw in the dining room? A man who was ashen, balding, and sick beyond comprehension at age 25.

The incident with my uncle had a profound impact on me as a child but has also afflicted me well into my adult life. A seed of a fear had been planted in my mind and just like any other fear, it grew and spread almost unnoticed for years. What had been a fear of a violent uncle slowly became a fear that I would become like him.

The nature of his illness and the cause of his outbursts were never explained to me as a child. I felt powerless, and as a result, my imagination filled in the blanks. Not knowing any better, I adopted the belief that what he had was contagious.

I have memories of walking past him and holding my breath and picking up my pace for fear of catching what he had. Looking back, I don't believe an explanation would have helped. I wouldn't have known what schizophrenia was. I would have just heard words like "hereditary" and "genetic predisposition" and the same fear would have taken on a new face. After all, he is my blood.

This idea that all diseases were contagious stayed with me into my adulthood. I can recall many a time when I would find myself holding my breath when faced with something that triggered that illogical fear. One day in Santa Monica, I was shopping with my oldest son, David, who was six at the time – an apple cider in hand, enjoying a gorgeous, fall day. As we walked past a homeless man chattering away to himself, I caught myself holding my breath until we had passed. Another time, I was in the midst of a twenty mile run; my heart was racing as I hit my stride. As I turned a corner and passed an intersection, I crossed paths with a homeless woman pushing a cart and talking loudly to herself. In the middle of a run, in the middle of intense cardio, I held my breath as I passed her.

Believe me, I know full well how utterly ridiculous it was to believe that mental illness, schizophrenia specifically, are things you can "catch." But this stands as a testament to the power of illogical fear. Without acknowledgement, these fears continue to live and grow. My fear of schizophrenia was masking my real fear. What I actually feared was the unpredictable, indescribable, uncontrollable nature of life. I wouldn't know it for many years, but luckily, the realization would be one that saved my life.

CHAPTER 6:

Anorexia –

I Don't Have To Eat

When I was 12 years old, I remember a balmy summer evening walking home after dinner from a quaint, local Italian restaurant with my sister, then 16. To say I thought the world of her would have been the understatement of my life. She was in high school, was cool and popular, and carried herself with an air of quiet self-assuredness. I felt special that she would even want to go out to dinner with me and elect to spend time with me. I loved being with her, and she embodied so many of the things that, at that time I aspired to be.

At 12, I was still a child in so many ways. On this particular evening, I was wearing little shorts with a tank top so I could stay cool in the summer heat and spring into cartwheels whenever I saw fit. As we headed home, my sister walked behind me and I skipped and ran ahead. I was small and spritely, always energetic and playful. I would often interchange my steps from walking, skipping, and running. As we approached our block, I sprinted for the front door. When she caught up with me, she spun around with a quiet regard and said, "I can see it's starting; you're beginning to get cellulite on the back of your thighs. You need to start watching what you eat." She pointed at my legs to punctuate her observation.

Cellulite?

I tried to make sense of what she had said. I was starting to get cellulite? I didn't even fully know what that meant but it sounded like something I didn't want. I realize now how ridiculous the statement was, especially since at the time I hadn't even gone through puberty. My figure was that of a tomboy at best, not even a suggestion of a curve in sight. I was overcome with worry. All I could think was, "How do I stop this? Does this mean I'm going to be overweight?" I ran straight into the house and into the bathroom to further inspect my thighs in the mirror. I searched for any indication of the "changes" my sister had seen. It was the very first time I worried about my weight. Another seed of fear was planted, and as we now understand about fear, that seed began to grow roots.

Five years later, I developed an eating disorder. As I sat reminiscing about that night, I acknowledged that it certainly was a moment that bore great impact. I don't believe my sister said it to hurt or belittle me. In fact, I think if she had known just how much it would hurt me, she would have refrained from saying anything in the first place.

Through my work with Something for Kelly, a foundation that advocates for education, empowerment, and awareness for individuals with eating disorders, I have shared that anorexia is a disease that can be triggered by a handful of outside factors. Just hearing a few words and internalizing that fear and confusion was the beginning of my struggle.

New scientific findings are proving that eating disorders and other heritable diseases are catalyzed by a number of factors, the top three being dysfunctional family dynamics, feelings of exclusion in social groups, and negative external influences. External influences would include the impossible and unrealistic portrayal of women's bodies on the covers of every women's magazine. It's safe to say that almost all of us have experienced one or more of these three factors. Though my sister's remark was what I remember, there were many other uncontrollable factors that contributed to my experience.

My first bout with anorexia occured at seventeen when I ate almost nothing for an entire week. All of my friends were going away to college and beginning to live more independently. I was staying home for college and felt sad and left behind. Up to that point my parents had strict parameters around when I could leave the house and who I could spend my time with. Although I know their overprotectiveness was born of the desire to keep me safe, I still felt left behind. Before they were to leave, five of my closest girlfriends and I were going to spend spring break week of senior year in Hawaii. I was so excited about the trip, but also felt dread. This trip brought home the realization that everything was about to change. Instead of working through that worry, I put all that energy into what I would look like in a bathing suit.

I felt a mounting pressure. I wasn't overweight; in fact, I was a size four. My issues with food never began as a desire to lose weight; I had always been a healthy and consistent weight. I was very active and participated in gymnastics, ballet, and tap. But my life was beginning to feel out of control. I didn't think anything of forgoing food; it was my body and I could control it.

In that week I lost seven pounds. When I got home after the trip, and the emphasis of "things never being the same" subsided, I went right back to eating normally. This was the first warning sign, one we all missed. Eating disorders weren't prevalent among my family or friends, and I didn't really understand what anorexia was. All I did know was that feeling in control of my body gave me a sense of control over my life.

Food quickly became nothing more than something I could control. In fact, I felt like I gained strength from not desiring it at all, to be able to dictate when I decided to eat versus eating as a reaction to my body's hunger. This was my attempt to take back control. Because I couldn't control my life, I felt shame and undeserving of good things. I believed I deserved the very minimum in every way and food played heavily into that belief. I couldn't see the complete correlation between feeling undeserving and not eating. Put simply, I felt so emotionally empty inside that I made myself physically empty. This isn't a logical way of thinking, which is why it is a disorder.

I can still remember my daily eating regimen.

BREAKFAST

I would have one cup of black coffee with sweet and low, half a grapefruit or cut papaya, followed by a two-hour workout.

LUNCH

A large bottle of water – a 1.5-liter Crystal Geyser, which I carried everywhere I went. On days when I felt I would pass out on the freeway driving back home from college, I would have a date or a few raisins.

DINNER

Steamed vegetables (usually Brussels sprouts) or vegetable soup, with no oil.

This desire to gain control resulted in a five-year battle with anorexia and body dysmorphia. It was the darkest and heaviest time I had ever experienced up to that point. I felt alone, lost, and without a clue as to who I was.

I have never believed that anyone was meant to live a life of unhappiness, even during that time of my life, and yet I did not hold that same belief for myself. I didn't feel that I deserved love or happiness; therefore, I didn't give myself the permission or the voice to express those desires. Instead, the constant refrain in my head was: "How dare I ask for anything?" This is the voice of shame. Shame is the fear that if people knew something about you then they would no longer love or accept you. Shame is feeling undeserving; that if we behave in a certain way then we will no longer be deserving of love.

This was how I felt all the time. I felt shame for myself, my body, and about my decision not to eat because I knew I should be putting my energy into something more important.

I had a daily ritual. I would go into the bathroom, and conduct a pinch-test, grabbing bits of skin between my thumb and index finger to ensure I had no fat deposits. Sometimes I did this more than once a day and, if I'm honest, I did this anytime I passed by a mirror in private. It was a thorough investigation I performed, making sure there were no signs of fat or cellulite. No signs of shame. I examined my body intensely and yet I still could not see what harm I was doing to my body. Healing cannot happen until you acknowledge the problem. It wasn't going to happen for me until I could clearly see what I was doing. Fortunately, I did one fateful morning.

I was in the midst of my morning pinch-test investigation when I caught sight of my reflection in the mirror. My real reflection. A skeletal, unrecognizable stranger stared back at me. I was horrified. I looked for the person I knew myself to be and couldn't find her. I broke into a sweat and started to panic. I screamed for my mother at the top of my lungs, "MOM, MOM, COME MOM!" My poor mother. Her own nerves were shot because she worried the damage I was doing to my body would be irreversible. I was shocked by what I had done to myself. It was the first time I could see the devastation I had caused. The skeletal woman in the mirror had been created by no one else but me. Finally, my healthy fear had arrived.

I had been standing on a high ledge, my toes dangling off the edge, for five straight years. The same fear I had as a child of the unknown, of life's unpredictability, the uncontrollable, had caught up with me again. As I saw myself in the mirror that day, my healthy fear saved me. It kicked in. And I stepped back.

CHAPTER 7:

David – I'm Still

Not In Control

Two years after I recovered from anorexia, I became pregnant with my first child and oldest son, David. For the first time in a long time I didn't fear food and I gave into my body's desires. Although the growing and changing shape of my body was uncomfortable, I had the awareness it was for something far greater. This was the first letting go in the process of becoming a mother. The next challenge was labor – something I refused to think about until I was going into labor.

At 24 years old, I thought I would just waltz into the hospital. I expected to be in pain for a little while, to push, feel some discomfort, push more, and then, just like that, he'd be born. Just like it happens in the movies. I can almost hear the mothers out there giggling at my naiveté. Anyone who has ever given birth knows that it isn't something you waltz into – or out of.

The reality was that I was in labor for 23 hours, 22 of which I had contractions pretty consistently every minute. In all that time, I had only dilated to 1 cm, and hadn't become any closer to giving birth. I had committed myself to a natural birth and wasn't going to budge from that decision, but life had other plans. By the 18th hour, I was so exhausted I was passing out between contractions. My OBGYN recommended an epidural, but I continued to resist. I also continued to pass out. Finally, completely depleted of any energy, I accepted the medication.

As my friend's grandmother has shared with me, "There is absolutely no need to worry while you're in labor, because let me tell you a secret, the baby always comes out in the end." Unfortunately, this advice doesn't really tell you much about the process.

Throughout my life, up to and including this point, I kept trying to control things I feared. The experience of birthing David was the first time I surrendered myself to something completely out of my control. Whenever I was face-to-face with something I feared, I tried to control, ignore or run away from it. I had no out; I had no options, David had to come out. In my mind having the epidural was a type of surrender, but as you'll see, that's not the surrender I've come to understand.

CHAPTER 8:

Joshua – My Body
Has Betrayed Me

I had a long held, mistaken belief that if you're on a spiritual path nothing bad can happen to you. Spirituality isn't a security blanket. It offers no guarantee that nothing "bad" will happen, it doesn't hide you from harm or protect you from life. It doesn't stop your process from occurring.

Spirituality doesn't save you from difficulty; it guides you through experiences so you can learn and grow from them. As I've shared, my fear always manifested out of feeling as though I wasn't in control, fearing the unknown. I grew exponentially in my ability to trust. To have trust in the Creator, to have certainty that everything was unfolding for my greatest good.

One of my biggest, life-changing moments occurred when my second son, Josh was born. The pregnancy had been difficult and Josh's birth was complicated, culminating in an emergency C-section. I had felt a lot of doubt and fear throughout the pregnancy. I bled for the first three months, nearly miscarried, and I showed much less than with my first pregnancy. In fact, I remained small enough for people to comment on it - and often. With each passing month, instead of being excited for the day I would meet my new child, I was overcome with unease. Intuitively, I knew my life would change forever and not in the ways one would anticipate after giving birth.

Josh's delivery was in every way different from my experience with David. This time, I began in fear. I couldn't stop the anxious feelings that something was going to go wrong. My hopes for a natural birth were dashed again. My C-section was scheduled for 7 a.m. and as I was rolled on my hospital bed, I half expected to find the delivery room to be an arena theatre with faceless medical students taking notes. Everything was bright, fluorescent, cold; the air was sterile and biting. Doctors and nurses moved with intention in every direction, talking about golf and the weather.

A partition went up at my chest, blocking my sight of anything happening below. Everything felt wrong. I felt fuzzy and lightheaded. I tried to speak and couldn't. Michael, my husband, was with me as they cut my body open. I felt like the dissected frog in a fifth grade science class. I was vulnerable. My mind was foggy and I was desperately trying to keep myself aware and understand what was happening.

Finally, a small warm bundle was placed on my chest. I felt a wash of relief. But then he was taken from me. Why can't I hold him longer? I heard my doctor say, "Oh, Monica, this has been the problem all along. Look how thin the umbilical cord is. That's why you were so small for the past eight months."

In recovery, I finally began to feel hopeful about the future for the first time in eight months. The fog was lifting and I was slowly coming back to my senses. I learned later that I had been given morphine and my fogginess and subsequent discomfort were the result. I felt relief. The surgery was over, my epidural was wearing off, and my newborn baby was sleeping sweetly in his crib beside me. It was a chaotic experience, but as I lay in the bed on the other side of it, I rested into the thought it had all unfolded perfectly. The trepidation I had felt during the pregnancy was now behind me. And then there was a knock at the door.

It was an associate of my pediatrician, who had an uncanny resemblance to Robin Williams' character in the movie Patch Adams. I was happy to see him and to finally have a conversation about my new baby. He asked where my husband was and I replied that he had gone to get David. I continued to explain how David had waited so long for a sibling, he had been begging me for a year, and he was beyond excited to meet his new baby brother. "Unfortunately, it can't wait," he replied.

"My husband should be back in about ten minutes or so," I said. Instantly I knew something was wrong. He went on to say, without skipping a beat, "We are 99% sure that your son has Down Syndrome." My heart started pumping, my palms began to sweat, and instinctively, my flight response kicked in. I wanted to jump off of the bed and run out of the room.

A trap door opened up between my ribs and my heart fell right through it.

It all began to make sense. I had spotted two months into pregnancy, I had been consistently cramping and bleeding. Everyone remarked about how small I was. I didn't even look pregnant. I couldn't exercise without becoming violently ill. With David, I ran every day well into the last months and then lap swam in the final weeks. With Josh, I couldn't. The day I became pregnant with Josh was the day everything changed. Somewhere inside of me I knew that something so profound was happening that it made me take pause. It felt like I was holding my breath until it felt safe to breathe again. The feelings of shock gave way to a feeling of total inadequacy and then crushing shame. I felt like I had failed. I failed him. I'd failed Michael. My body had betrayed me.

But why did it have to be his mind? Of all the things, of all the complications, of all the afflictions it might have been. Why his mind? I was my eight-year-old self again, afraid, wanting to cover my eyes and make it all disappear.

Two days after Josh's birth, a team of doctors sat Michael and me down to discuss Josh. They felt somehow we weren't fully comprehending Josh's diagnosis so they made it their duty to list all of the problems that Josh might have, each one of them a nightmare for any parent. The list of possible afflictions was long - he could possibly have a hole in his heart, he potentially would be susceptible to seizures, it would be years before he could attempt to eat solid food. That seemingly endless list was followed only by another list of the things he would never be able to do. Normal things that every kid deserves to do, like playing sports, living independently, or having a rich life full of joyous experiences.

It felt like they were asking us to give up anything positive associated with Josh. But really it felt like they were asking us to just give up. To give up on our son. We were 27 and 28, and terrified. Josh was only just born, he had only been in the world for 48 hours, and this was how we were meeting him. Uncertainty and fear pumped through me as fully as oxygen. I couldn't even imagine what the rest of our lives would look like. But, I remember thinking: I have a choice. I can either feed into the fear of the reality the doctors were positing, I could give in to my own fears about what raising a child with Down Syndrome would do to me and my family, or I could be attuned to the beauty and potential of what he could become - and subsequently, who I would become.

Today he is 15. He's happy and healthy and living life as his best self.

The anxiety and subsequent panic that I experienced during my pregnancy and delivery with Josh was overwhelming at times. It was something entirely new to me; it felt bigger than me in every way. I had faced challenges before and though they involved fear, I had a degree of confidence in my tools and my ability. This time, I didn't know what to do. What worked for me before wasn't working now. The anxiety eventually grew into desperation and finally, I had to let go. I had to accept what was because I had no other choice.

In regard to Josh, many of the things I feared never came to pass. And so it is with life. The things we fear usually never come true; it's the ones we never give thought to or deem possible that really get us. At the time, I felt I was in limbo waiting to find out test results or waiting to have more answers about him, about how to raise him, about what to expect, about what I should do. I was even worried about puberty, something so far down the road.

I was given the chance to put my certainty to the test and let go.

Certainty looks like this: I feel uncomfortable. I don't know what to do. I've exercised every option. I trust this process completely because I trust the Creator completely and I know that all that happens is ultimately in my best interest.

Instead of waiting to know exactly how he would turn out, I decided to choose how I wanted to live in each moment and give voice to that desire instead of my fears. Through the early months after his birth, I realized we never know how anyone will turn out. Who, after all, is typical? I just happened to find out about Josh's limitations the day of his birth but, I have his entire lifetime to discover his gifts. Most experience life the other way around. I realized we all have processes in our life and that is the purpose. So, instead of waiting for answers, I decided to let go of all the fear and embrace Josh. This process didn't happen overnight, but rather with the passage of time, introspective thought, and a commitment to seeing beauty in what is most challenging and having certainty in that process.

Hearing what we heard from our doctors that day could have filled us with a fear powerful enough to break us down and break us apart. Even so, while it seemed like a real fear, it wasn't. It was worry, which is a byproduct of fear and offers just as little service. It gives the illusion of action while actually getting you nowhere. It may feel as though you are doing something by worrying about the issue, but you aren't moving forward – neither away from fear nor toward anything better. As Corrie Ten Boom said, "Worrying does not empty tomorrow of its troubles, it empties today of its strength." I read this quote every day for the first three months of Josh's life.

CHAPTER 9:

Miriam – True Surrender

Josh's diagnosis had given me the opportunity to make a choice. A choice to release fear and fully embrace what was. I let go of my fear and my anxiety and stepped into surrender. However, even though I had made the choice, even though I now had this new consciousness, my mind and body needed time to catch up. After Josh, I was traumatized and though I had a new understanding, I was crippled with fear. I may have made the decision to embrace what was, but I carried the residue of my recent experience. My adrenal glands were shot because of all the stress I was under and I was devoid of any successful coping mechanisms. I didn't recognize this new version of myself.

During this time, in conversations I would reference things as "Before Josh" and "After Josh." That was how much my world had been turned upside down. Before I had Josh, I felt like I was secure and courageous. I loved to be dared to do outrageous and out-of-the-box things. For instance, among my cousins and younger sister I was the go-to person to pull out baby teeth. I was the one who always remained cool, calm, and collected in the midst of chaos. Nothing fazed me. I didn't mind blood and I gravitated toward anything wild or scary. Then Josh arrived. Suddenly the sight of blood made me faint. It was indescribably strange to have been a certain way for 27 years of my life only to find myself in another reality that was altogether different.

I recall one particular night, I heard a thump, followed by a yelp and the pitter patter of footsteps running into my bedroom. In the darkness, I greeted my son David mid-run. He said he fell and bumped his head. I brought him to my chest and held him close, then tucked him into my bed. I walked into the bathroom, turned the light on, and to my horror, my white shirt was covered in blood.

My heart started racing, my breath became short, and, since I was half asleep, I lifted up my shirt to see where the blood was coming from, searching my body to find the source. When I found nothing, I realized it was coming from David.

I turned on the light and found my bed covered in blood and an opening in David's forehead from which blood was streaming out. I would later come to find that David had a fright in the night and was running to our room for comfort. In the dark, his foot got tangled in his blankets thrusting him forward into the corner of his half-open door, splitting his forehead.

Upon realizing the severity of his wound, I woke Michael and he went downstairs with David to get him ready to go to the hospital for stitches. Then my vision began to blur, my eyes filled with black, and I fainted. It's a stroke of luck that I didn't end up needing stitches, too.

My fainting episode made me realize how far fear had taken me. I had become a fear-based person, which was not my personality! And I asked myself, "Wait, is this who you are now? And how much more fearful will you become as you grow older?"

Needless to say, when baby three came along, fear and uncertainty came along with her.

I got pregnant with my daughter three months after Josh was born. I intentionally got pregnant again quickly, because I knew that if I didn't I would have let my fears around the pregnancy with Josh, as well as his birth, overwhelm me. I likely just wouldn't have had any more kids. It was the bravest thing I have ever done.

My previous experience had not only been traumatic, but there is an increased chance that after one Down Syndrome birth the following child could have Down Syndrome, as well. I knew I couldn't allow this fear into my experience and that it was up to me to connect to certainty.

Because my previous experience was so troubling, I began a search for a new doctor and, with it, a new experience. Nothing that happened was my previous doctor's fault, but there were certain things I felt could have been handled differently along the way. One example: just after I'd received Josh's diagnosis, I heard someone in the hallway whistling the tune, "Zippity-doo-da." It stopped and my OBGYN entered. We spoke briefly about Josh and then he left the room. The door had barely closed behind him before he picked up the tune, and continued whistling. I felt a distinct lack of empathy. Later, during my pregnancy with Miriam, every time I saw his name appear across my phone whenever he would call me, my heart would drop, and I would prepare myself for bad news. Not a healthy reaction to have when your doctor is calling you.

A couple of my friends provided me with some referrals - each one worse than the last. The first doctor I saw was so old, I was concerned he might retire (or die) before I gave birth. The second smelled of onions and I couldn't bear to be in his office. The third doctor, by far the most entertaining, albeit at my expense, had a strange preoccupation with glass, plastic, and ceramic frog figurines. Upon walking into her office I saw hundreds of large and small frogs covering any space available–floor, walls, and ceiling housed these amphibian collectibles. I even recall her wearing a frog pendant. It struck me as interesting at first, almost endearing. Unfortunately, they were deceptive.

We sat down and I began to describe my history, how many kids I had. I told her about my very recent experience surrounding Josh's delivery, and then I told her I was four weeks pregnant with my third child. She looked me dead in the eyes and, in her thick accent, without skipping a beat replied, "You, with your SH!T LUCK, why you have more baby? No. No more baby for you."

My husband shot out of his chair in a fit of laughter and headed for the door; he didn't need to hear any more, while I sat stunned, slack jawed and stuck to my seat. Clearly she had misunderstood me. Carefully articulating my words, speaking much more slowly, I said to her, "No, I don't think you understand, I'm ALREADY four weeks pregnant." Pointing at my belly to reiterate, "I am pregnant right now."

"No, no. No more baby for you," she said more emphatically – her frog pendant eyeballing me as if to further her point. I decided right then and there my previous doctor wasn't so bad. It took the search, with its entertaining, yet unceremonious end, to realize my original doctor was a great doctor and we had a lot of history together. However, an honest conversation was also needed and I wanted to give him the chance to decide if he could be the doctor I needed him to be.

I told him that while I didn't blame him or hold him responsible for what happened I did not like the way he handled the surprising diagnosis with Josh and that his actions and words had lacked empathy. I went on to say that I was still raw from this experience – especially since it had only been three months since Josh's birth. Now I was preparing for another nine months of uncertainty (or so I felt at the time) and if he wanted to remain my doctor I would need him to be present. It was, after all, just as much his choice. But it was necessary for him to clearly understand what I needed.

I also explained to him I would probably call him often with ridiculous questions and unsubstantiated worries and would likely be more nervous and high strung than before. If he couldn't be the kind of doctor I felt I needed, then I wanted to know. He accepted all I said and appreciated that I shared my feelings and fears with him. He actually thanked me for being so honest, and although he didn't say it, I think he liked that he was being asked to be accountable. I, in turn, felt relief. From there, I was able to focus on the child growing inside of me.

I began speaking to her. I told her every day when she was in utero how things were going to be. You are strong and healthy. You will come into the world with ease and grace.

Well, apparently Miriam had a mind of her own, even then, so she didn't really follow my "ease and grace" instruction. Miriam is very sure about what she likes and how she likes things to be done. When I was nearly two weeks past due, we were having frequent checkups and on one such visit our doctor said, if you don't give birth in two days, we are going to need to induce you. That's all Miriam had to hear, and just like that, as we were leaving the doctor's office, I started to go into soft labor. Immediately, the fear settled in.

The next morning when I started to go into active labor, Michael and I arrived at the hospital, but my doctor wasn't there yet. As fear started to take the front seat and my rational brain was becoming muted, I began pleading with Michael in the parking garage that it was better to leave and go home for a bit. The doctor wasn't even there, we could just come back later. I wasn't thinking straight and although I knew I couldn't walk away from labor, I was going to try and delay it. He convinced me to get out of the car, convinced me to stay in the waiting room, but after a while longer, I decided I was leaving. I made it halfway down the hall when I heard my doctor's voice over my shoulder saying, "Where do you think you're going?" I accepted in that moment there was no escape.

I was in labor for eighteen hours. My mentors, who were also, by the grace of God, my parents-in-law, Rav and Karen Berg were there, offering love, support, and prayer. They wanted to be there for me – especially after the recent experience I had with Josh. But it was right before the holiday of Shavuot and thousands of Kabbalah Centre students from all over the world who were attending services were already at the hotel, which was a two-hour drive without traffic. To make matters worse, the pressing event was due to start in four hours. The clock was ticking and this only served to add an additional pressure of time.

Miriam, true to her form, had other ideas and labor stalled. My plans for a natural birth were once again dashed as the medical team administered a dose of Pitocin, an aid in inducing labor. I thought I knew very well what pain was after my first two labors, but that drug is like a train cutting through you at maximum speed. The pain was blinding. Almost immediately, they gave me something else, something that made me feel serene but also fuzzy. I looked to Michael. He was distracted and his eyes were filled with concern, he checked my monitors intensely and the anesthesiologist was throwing things off shelves in a frantic search for something. In my state of mind at the time, I found that amusing, as if I were watching a film.

Later, I was told that my heart rate and my daughter's heart rate had dropped dangerously low. At this point, through the haze of medications, I was at a place that felt like a dead-end and in that I found a gentle clarity. I knew that the assistance I needed was going to come from somewhere far greater than a doctor, anesthesiologist, or hospital. I looked up from my hospital bed to the ceiling and whispered to the Creator, "I'm yours, and I surrender to you completely. I trust you. Whatever should be, should be." I didn't want to leave this world that day, but I was ready for whatever was meant to be. I felt total certainty and trust.

Surrender is not about giving in or giving up. It is the act of not knowing an outcome and putting yourself in the hands of the Creator. *I am yours.*

It was the first time I experienced true surrender and it was the most blissful feeling of freedom I have ever felt in my life. I was no longer attached to anything; I wasn't ruled by anything, and I wasn't fearful of anything. I just was. It is the purest, highest expression to which we can aspire and it is available to us in every single moment. Two minutes into my surrender, Miriam was born.

Looking back, I see now that each of my pregnancies had given me new opportunities to eliminate fear and understand certainty even more deeply. I needed my experience with Josh, the fear and the anxiety, in order to truly let go. That desperation and exhaustion forced me to let go, to step into surrender for the first time. Miriam's birth was my opportunity to experience that surrender in action.

As we work toward eliminating fear, we can understand it takes time. It takes dedication. When we decide to remove fear, it doesn't just vanish, we have to work consistently to remove it.

CHAPTER 10:

Abigail –

Becoming A Channel

At this point, you may think I'm a glutton for punishment to go a fourth round. However, for all the ways I know pregnancy and labor to be the most difficult of experiences, I also know that having children is the most worthwhile endeavor, to experience life at every stage, being a part of the creation of a life, in the fullest sense, from beginning to end.

Having had my first three children in my 20's, I was a different person by the time I was in my 30's, my late 30's at that. I was in a completely different place spiritually, emotionally, mentally, and physically – I believe all of these factors enabled me to finally have the birth experience I had envisioned, but this time without fear.

After all, with Miriam I had come so close, even though it may not have gone exactly the way I had hoped. Maybe it was a lack of certainty or lack of a plan or maybe I just hadn't found my strongest connection to the Creator, but I was oh so close. If I am honest with myself, I hadn't confidently decided, nor had I come to a place of certainty that I could give birth naturally and without any medical intervention. And, if there is anything I know for sure, it is that in life, nothing happens until you decide. Childbirth is life's perfect workshop for this exact principle.

It takes you nine months to grow your baby and prepare your body and mind for labor and delivery. Every day you can decide how you want to experience your pregnancy. Then the time comes to deliver. You push and nothing happens. You wait, and wait some more. Maybe there's a complication, something is taking longer than expected. Then, it's time again. You push again and again, but still nothing. When do you step away? You don't, because it's not an option – the baby needs to come out. Sometimes you continue pushing, sometimes you have to change course (cesarean or another intervention). But either way you don't stop working towards the end goal. You are all in. Giving up is not an option. The only option given to you in this moment is found in your free will. It is exercised in choosing how you want to experience it. Events may not be in our control, but we can control our reaction – for instance, choosing certainty instead of fear. The most important choice.

With my fourth pregnancy, I deliberately worked to let go of the fear I had surrounding the other pregnancies. When I let go of fear, I opened myself up to experiences and realizations that I wouldn't have had otherwise. Because each pregnancy was so different and I uncovered new tools each time, I finally found myself right where I had always wanted to be. Without my fear, I was able to have an even more beautiful experience than I could have expected. I chose to connect to my baby growing inside me. This choice gave me the understanding that neither the pregnancy nor her delivery was about me or my experience. Nor was it about my body, my discomfort, or my pain. Rather, it was about her evolution, her experience, and how she would enter the world. When I came to this realization, I decided to facilitate a birth for her that would be positive and free of stress. I was the channel for which she would come into the world, but it was her journey.

I put together a plan that fully readied my mind, body, and spirit. I had the support of a doula, I clearly communicated with all involved in the birth about my vision for the delivery I wanted, and I placed total trust in the Creator. And although I had a plan, I was willing to accept any outcome.

With all my heart and soul, those nine months of carrying her became more about the moment of her birth than anything else. When it was time for her to make her entry into the world, I continued to focus on creating the most pleasant experience for her. I thoughtfully and carefully prepared for the day of her delivery and I was able to have the natural hypno-birth I had always envisioned. Not only because I wanted it that way, but because it's what Abigail wanted and needed.

As my husband and I counted contractions, the pain changed in its intensity. The first ten seconds were tolerable, then there were 10-20 and 20-30 seconds where I was in a state of OMG OUCH; and then there were 30-40 seconds where the pain was tolerable again. When I exercise, I get through the pain because I know that I won't be in it forever. Labor became just like exercise, everything was mind over matter. The pain of conditioning my body and mind with extreme workouts and marathon training prepared me for the physical feat of delivering my daughter. I told myself, "I know I can endure anything for 40 seconds, as long as I know the pain will come to an end. I can get my head around it." In life we fight discomfort but when we embrace the uncomfortable things, they pass much more quickly and pain is an energy that can be converted. Pain is a force, it's strong, overwhelming, even debilitating, but when we take this great force and use its strength for our designated outcome, in this case bringing a child into the world in a peaceful way, pain is converted to power.

It may seem as if you can save yourself pain by avoiding difficulty. We often fight uncomfortable things. We fight our process and we fight our circumstances. I tried to do just that for many years. Next time you find yourself in emotional or physical pain, don't try to go around it or avoid it; work through it instead.

I never said a single word during the eight hours of labor, six of which were at home. The first words I uttered when she came out and was placed upon my stomach were "I'm so proud of you. What a great job you did. You are strong and healthy and beautiful and I love you." I wanted the first words she ever heard in her life to be how great she is, powerful, beautiful, and complete.

Abigail is such a blessing and brings me joy every single day. I can think of nothing more worthwhile than the work of bringing a child into the world. It was certainly worth it to find the support and strategies that allowed me to push my fear of labor out of my life so Abigail could come into it in the most positive way possible.

No energy is ever wasted, and life, in a nutshell, is just experience. We can draw on what we've gained, no matter where we have learned the lesson, whenever we need it. You'll begin to see that everything in life prepares you for something else, if you are paying attention.

With Miriam's birth I fully trusted the Creator. However, with Abigail's birth I not only trusted in the Creator, but I was one with the Creator. I felt like His worker, doing His work.

CHAPTER 11:

Fear Is Not An Option

Late one evening, when Miriam was an infant, I was breastfeeding her and my tongue started tingling. I could then feel the tingle slowly starting in my fingers and legs, as well. It spread to my entire body and was so overwhelming that I started to panic. And I mean, really panic – that feeling of drowning, a total loss of logic or reason, an anxiety so debilitating I felt like I couldn't breathe.

Once again, my old fear of being out of control showed up.

Michael and I called his parents, the Rav and Karen, on the phone and by the sound of my voice they could tell that I was scared. Karen tried to talk to me logically about what could be happening while the Rav was telling me everything was okay.

Don't worry. But I wasn't responding and the Rav began to yell into my ear: "Monica, do you hear me? Fear is not an option!" I can still hear his voice in my head. Over and over again he said it. The Rav had unwavering determination and his perseverance was unmatched by anyone I have ever met. He got through to me. My panic began to recede. To this day, every time something comes up and I start to slip into a panic mode, I hear the Rav's voice saying, "Fear is not an option!"

I later found out the tingling was caused by doing an advanced Ashtanga yoga pose I had no business doing and that I had temporarily injured myself. Nothing serious or fear-inducing at all. Soon, I was fine and the tingling subsided. But, it is clear fear played absolutely no part in helping me get through it.

Feeding the fear doesn't serve us, it doesn't help us, and it doesn't change the situation.

It fuels an already chaotic situation and makes it worse. It doesn't change the reality of what is, or what's going to be, or what should be. It doesn't do anything but paralyze us. By meeting it head on, the fear you have can be cut down to size and its power taken away. It then makes room for courage, connecting to your strength, because then you know what you're made of.

PART 3:
How You Can Live
Fearlessly

CHAPTER 12:

Consciousness For

Living Fearlessly

My journey through fear has been a road crafted specifically to me and my purpose. We all have strengths that are shown through challenges and each of them is designed to help us become our truest, most fully realized self. It is the path to our purpose. Now that we have identified the three types of fear; healthy, real, and illogical, and have taken a look at how fear has shown up in my life, we can delve more deeply into understanding the fears in your life, and with tools and consciousness, help you eliminate them. The ultimate goal is to transcend fear and come to a place where you trust the Creator and the process of your life.

FIXED VS. GROWTH MINDSET

There are two basic mindsets we fall into that shape our lives. In a fixed mindset, your abilities, intelligence, and talents are static. Like a computer program that is loaded into your brain at birth, it runs involuntarily and remains the same. In a growth mindset, those same abilities, intelligence, and talents are honed and strengthened through learning and experience. A growth mindset is geared toward constant evolution and a fixed mindset is geared toward constant validation. Much of our understanding of this concept comes from the work of renowned Stanford psychologist Carol Dweck.[4]

The hallmark difference between these two mindsets is that one views failure as devastation and the other sees failure as an opportunity.

As you begin a path of uncovering and eliminating your fears, ask yourself: "What mindset am I operating from?" If you're not sure, take a look at the list of qualities for each:

Fixed
- Avoids challenges
- Finds obstacles to be overwhelming, prone to giving up
- Views effort as fruitless
- Is defensive or ignores negative feedback
- Feels threatened by the success of others

Growth
- Embraces challenges
- Persists in the face of setbacks
- Views effort as the path to success
- Learns from and integrates feedback
- Finds lessons and inspiration from the success of others[5]

If you find yourself resonating with the fixed mindset do not fret, in fact, get excited! Switching the gears from fixed to growth requires only an openness and willingness to do so. Within a fixed mindset, the beliefs around what is possible for you are extremely limited and based in fear. Fear of appearing inadequate, unintelligent, irresponsible, unworthy. As you work to remove those fears, you'll automatically adopt a growth mindset and along with it, a new perspective, which is where our work of eliminating fear begins.

YOU'RE NOT UNLUCKY, YOU'RE FEARFUL

Fear feeds off stagnation and blocks us from being our best. It keeps us from taking advantage of the opportunities that present themselves to us. Sometimes these opportunities are labeled "miracles" or "luck" but nothing just falls in your lap. You need to be open to receive, and if fear is present it can block you from not only realizing your full abilities but from any opportunity that comes your way.

Fortunately, we have more control over our lives than we realize.

Most people would not equate missed opportunities with fear. We have adopted a very strange perception that opportunities are all about luck when in fact, it is often fear that stops us from seeing those opportunities.

We adopt this mindset because it's easier to blame lack of circumstance than to do the work of removing fear, and thereby changing our reality. All this "lucky" versus "unlucky" thinking gets in our way. Luck is a state of mind, it is a way of thinking. Luck is not a magical ability or a gift from God. Remember the story about placing pennies over our eyes?

When we are distracted and overwhelmed by our fears we are blinded to the opportunities that exist all around us.

Further, it states in the Zohar that "good" and "bad" luck are simply codes for the principle of cause and effect.

Michael Berg states, "We create our own luck through our behavior and interactions with other people. Actions that are selfish, abusive, or inconsiderate propagate misfortune in our lives, which we mistakenly interpret as bad luck."

Don't settle for the idea that you are an unlucky person. Let this understanding empower you, knowing that you have the potential to be great – and greatness entails a commitment to yourself to overcome challenges and not be overcome by them.

THE POWER OF PERSPECTIVE

We always have a choice. That choice begins with perspective. From there, we can begin to change our words, actions, and ultimately, our experience. The power of perspective is undeniable, and as you learn more about your own, you will begin to understand the power of your choices.

Take a look at this series of words:
opportunityisnowhere

Did you read *opportunity is now here*?
Or *opportunity is nowhere?*

One person can read this and see an encouraging message while another can read the exact opposite. On a grander scale, those who allow fear to dominate them have a skewed perspective and thus, do not notice opportunities when they come. This is the power of perspective.

How do your fears stop you from achieving and accomplishing things you want in your life?

What kind of shift can you make in terms of your perspective?

A quick way to see a situation differently is by answering two questions:

If you removed your fear, how would your reality change?

What would you do today if you had no fear?

Now act on that.

MIND, BODY & SPIRIT: APPLYING A SHIFTED PERSPECTIVE

Once you understand your perspective and how you can shift it, you can begin to anchor the new view by making small changes. I came up with a three-step action plan that can work for you as you begin to move away from fear and toward that which you truly want. First, I will share how I used these tools when I delivered Abigail as an example:

Mind

Because fear begins in the mind, I took steps to ensure that my focus could be directed positively. Applying what I had learned from my past pregnancies, I found someone who could be my voice during the delivery so that all of my concentration was on the task at hand so I mentally set myself up for success. For instance, a surgeon wouldn't take phone calls or walk out in the middle of surgery to get himself a cup of coffee. Likewise, all my attention needed to be on my mental state and Abigail's experience. I took hypno-birthing classes and learned about successful alternative births. I chose a doula whom I shared my history with and knew that the last thing I wanted was to feel like a science experiment. When an intern entered my room, an Ashton Kutcher lookalike wearing cowboy boots, my doula politely sent him away and I didn't have to utter a word. Find an advocate, someone you trust. When you head into a fear-filled situation consider finding an advocate or trusted friend who can offer support, as well as speak for you if you aren't able to do so for yourself.

Body

The second aspect is our physical body. One step I could take to ensure my body's comfort was wearing my own clothes throughout labor. It may seem inconsequential, but giving birth is about life and wearing a hospital gown subconsciously connected me to sickness and feeling out of control. I also stayed out of bed, because lying down was the opposite of my body's desire, and I needed gravity's help to bring the baby down. Instead, I moved and walked. I followed the signals that I was getting from my body, and as contractions came, I used them to continue to bring my baby a little further down the birth canal. Just because something is usually done in a certain way, doesn't mean that you have to do it that way. You have options. When overcoming your fears look at an expectation you may have that is connecting you to your fear, and change the rules.

Spirit

Finally, and most importantly, I placed total trust in the Creator. Whatever the outcome would be, I knew it was for the best, even if it didn't go as planned. Luckily, it did. I spent months working on my consciousness, but the real epiphany for me was when I was five days past my due date. I realized the labor is not my story or my experience, it's not even about my pain. It's about my child – her experience of coming into the world and traveling down the birth canal. It was her journey all along and I was just the vehicle to support her. Those nine months of carrying her became more about the moment of her birth. Ultimately, she arrived ten days later.

By nurturing those three important aspects, mind, body and spirit, I created the best experience for my daughter and me.

This Mind, Body, Spirit approach can be applied to other fears. For instance, if your fear is related to your career, or speaking up to an overbearing boss, partner, friend, or parent, you can apply these ideas to those unique experiences and challenges. Is there a person or situation with whom you have recurring conflict and fear of confrontation? We've all known that person who believes that if they say the most words the loudest that they've 'won' the discussion. The fear is understandable if the person in question has a great deal of power over your life, such as a boss.

Mind

See conflict as a means to find resolution, not to create animosity. It's easy to demonize another person's actions and views, but consider how things look from another's perspective.

In fraught conversations, one tool I like to use is to ask, rather than tell. Our brains react very differently when we hear a declarative statement versus a question. Declarative statements are processed and perhaps checked for veracity, and maybe pondered for a bit. Questions, however, send the brain on a search for possible solutions and recall memories of similar incidents that occurred with success in our pasts.

When confronted with a challenge, often we'll think, "Okay, I have this!" Researchers suggest to instead, ask yourself, "Okay, do I have this?" The interrogative self-talk is the better way to go and will yield better results than affirmative self-talk because the question prompts your brain to start looking for solutions.

Body

Dress in a way that makes you feel confident and powerful. Be well rested and perhaps, properly caffeinated. Stay connected to the person you are speaking to by mirroring their body language.

Spirit

Spirit is the same for every scenario, when you place your trust in the Creator the outcome may not be what you envisioned, but it will ultimately be for your greatest good.

FEAR OF THE UNKNOWN

Fear of the unknown is a universal experience. Before my husband and I relocated our family from Los Angeles to New York City we had endless conversations during which I had considered finding the right schools, a good neighborhood, and housing suitable for a large family.

Despite all of my planning, I was still met by the natural hurdles that come with living in a new place. Things I had taken for granted had now become a daily struggle. Making friends, for instance. I also hadn't considered how difficult it would be to find a new dentist, orthodontist, pediatrician, OBGYN, hairdresser, or any of the necessary things that support our lives. And then there were the murky fears that I couldn't even name such as how would I create a life without the support system on which I had so heavily relied? What would I do without family nearby?

At this point, after second-guessing and endless questioning, it became clear I could either let the fear dictate my future for me or I could just take the leap. If I stayed in LA, I knew how each day would unfold, more or less, one after the other, because I had lived there most of my life. I knew what my life was and what it would be. If I stayed, I would have been choosing comfort over curiosity, that would have been the safe choice.

But there is also no opportunity for growth within comfort.

As stated earlier, sometimes fear might not feel like fear. Staying in a predictable place isn't terrible, but when you go day-to-day, year-to-year without trying something new you are short-changing yourself. Though there is nothing wrong with comfort, it is always worth checking to be sure you aren't avoiding a higher calling. More to the point, it is only fear that stops us from opening a new book, starting a new chapter, and from creating a life that's different from the way we are living now. What often propels me to choose discomfort over comfort is asking myself this question:

Where do I want to see myself in five, ten, and 15 years?

I worked to tackle that fear of the unknown and two short months after giving birth to my fourth child, my husband and I made the decision to finally move our family of six across the country--three kids, three schools, and an infant in a new apartment not even half the size of our house in Los Angeles.

Do you choose comfort over curiosity?

In this moment, what is something you want to do?

What feels exciting to you or feels like it's part of who you're supposed to be?

Is fear playing a role in holding you back?

If you weren't afraid, what's the first thing you would do?

SHAME OF WANTING

One day, as I was leaving the house on my way to an appointment, I was pulling out of the driveway at the same time my eight year old daughter, Miriam, was being dropped off from school. I didn't see her as I pulled out and drove in the opposite direction, but she surely saw me.

I was on a call as I drove, then walked straight into my meeting upon arrival. Once the meeting ended and I was walking out, I looked at my phone and saw two voicemails from home. I listened and was met by a tiny voice filled with hysteria. It was Miriam. "MOMMY!" she managed to get out through hysterical gasps while trying to catch her breath, "I saw your car as we were driving in and then you just drove OFF! Did you SEE me? I was so excited that you were going to be home, there are so many things I wanted to tell you. Were you on your phone? When will you be home?" And then click, end of message.

As I listened to my daughter's message I was struck by something. She had called me to express, in the most pure and simple way, what she had hoped and wanted. She had wanted me to be home, plain and simple. There was no blame or malice in her message, she just expressed what she had desired. Not only that, it was completely uncorrupted by shame. It was innocent and true. This was a total revelation and gave me pause. How many of us are able to express our wants and true desires without feeling shame for wanting them in the first place?

It begs a very practical question: do we allow ourselves to ask for what we want?

Small children have no compunctions about asking for – even shrieking, as in Miriam's case – what they want. But at a critical point, somewhere during third, fourth, or fifth grade, the shame of wanting begins to set in. Shame is the fear that if someone really knows us, including our wants and desires, then they would no longer love us. We adopt the belief that it is impolite and socially unacceptable to ask for what we want and that we should wait until it's offered. Have you ever found yourself envying children for this? Sometimes I look at the rants and raves of small children and wish I could say, "I WANT THIS!" just as my daughter had expressed herself, untainted by social norms and preferences, and absent of shame or blame. For some reason, we do not express our wants because we become afraid of appearing too blunt, too aggressive, or too demanding or needy. But why is wanting something considered a bad thing? It isn't. It is the basic human condition to want, to desire, to dream. We owe it to ourselves to simply ask.

Most people live their lives in one of the following three realities. One is caring way too much about what people think. People with this mindset might be afraid to pursue the career they want, or marry the person they desire out of the fear their family won't approve. The second reality is repression. People in this category often explode out of frustration from repressing their true self, their true feelings, and from too often holding their tongue. After so many years of repressing their true desires, they become unkind to themselves and those closest to them. The third reality is one of resentment. This is when a person negates what they truly want, never allowing themselves to ask for more, because somewhere along the way they adopted the belief they can't have it.

There is absolutely no shame in wanting things and there should be no shame in asking for what we want. How else will people know what to give you if you don't ask? Desire, to dream. We owe it to ourselves to simply ask.

After that initial voicemail, another voicemail was waiting. Although Miriam's second call came an hour later, the voicemails played one after another. It was her again, completely calm, composed, and articulate. "Hi Mommy, I just called to tell you I love you and I hope that you're having a wonderful day. And I can't wait to see you!" I could almost hear her smile through the phone. In that moment my heart filled with so much love and pride for my child. More than that, in her beautiful eight-year-old wisdom she reminded me of a very basic and profound lesson. She had gathered herself, felt exactly what she needed to feel, expressed it, and felt no need to apologize for her perceived outburst. And just like that, it was done.

She didn't apologize, because there was no need to apologize. She was honest and true to herself in that moment. After some time passed, she used her words to express what was at the root of the first phone call. She wanted to spend time with me. What a gift. And because she had given herself the permission to express herself, she was able to move past the emotion very quickly. Every day I learn such incredible lessons from her and all my children.

As Oliver Wendell Holmes succinctly put it, "Pretty much all the honest truth-telling there is in the world is done by children."

FEAR OF FAILURE & REJECTION

Not all dreams come true. It's a hard fact of life and not one I would encourage anyone to dwell on because I do believe we can change our circumstances whenever we decide. We all know life is full of disappointments and dreams that didn't manifest. Instead, refocus all that energy into the next thing, the thing that is going to be possible because of the dream that never was. Energy is never wasted.

So many blessings and people come into our lives because of a change of course. We can't allow our failures to cause us so much fear that we don't try again.

"God blessed the broken road that led me straight to you,"[6] is a lyric from a Rascal Flatts song (country music is an entire genre devoted to setting heartbreak and disappointment to verse) and hits this nail directly on its head. Being from Louisiana, these songs touch a deep part of my essence.

I don't know about you, but my heart breaks a little for the athlete who has trained their whole life only to miss the Olympic team by one slot, for the bride left at the altar, and the friend who is so talented and yet just can't seem to catch a break. Rejection, especially public rejection, is an overwhelmingly negative feeling that often leads to a spiral of self-doubt. We've all been there, and some of us stay there for a very long time. We have had our hearts set on a particular job, been picked last for the team, shared something we wrote, ran for an office, or asked someone out on a date, and when we didn't get our desired outcome, our minds filled with awful rejection-fueled thoughts.

The simple definition of rejection is that someone declined what you offered. That doesn't sound so bad when put that way. Not everyone is going to value the same things you do. That's reasonable. Rejection doesn't mean that what you are offering isn't valuable or worthwhile; you just haven't yet found the right recipient. If you care less about what people think, you won't feel so rejected, because it's not personal. In fact, most rejection isn't personal at all. Yet, knowing all of this, why is rejection still so powerful and why does it have the ability to produce such negative emotions? It's your anterior cingulate cortex.

Neuroscientists have discovered that, unlike other kinds of emotions, intense rejection travels the same neural pathways as actual physical pain.

Scientists surmise that early on when a person was rejected from their family or tribe they were unlikely to survive on their own, therefore the brain developed a very intense warning system to dissuade us from behaviors that would lead to being ostracized. It turns out it works a little too well.

Even normally self-confident, well-adjusted, and emotionally stable people can question their sanity when assaulted with the negative emotions that come from rejection. Rejection can be so overwhelming; how are we expected to ever put ourselves out there again, fearing and risking more rejection? You aren't losing your mind, you aren't worthless, and you don't lack talent. Your brain is just running really old software that is trying to keep you from being cast out. It's really that ridiculous! Being armed with this knowledge can help lessen your distress the next time you get rejected – and if you are living life to the fullest, actively seeking your purpose, then you can bet there will be a next time.

Rejection can also be a powerful tool for motivation. Rejection can help us to take power from what could be a setback and use it to fuel our next charge. Russian Olympic figure skater, Yevgeny Plushenko, was interviewed after winning a gold medal at the Winter Olympics. Many questioned whether he'd even deserved a spot on the team. He was older than the other competitors and has undergone two knee surgeries and two spinal surgeries in the past two years. Many critics openly questioned his ability to perform. During his interview he was asked what he had to say to his critics in light of the gold medal he had just won. He looked straight into the camera and replied with a charming grin, "Thank you very much!" [7]

However, if you find yourself stuck in the rejection spiral, unable to use that rejection as fuel, there's always Tylenol. You heard me, the naturopath. Just as Tylenol dulls the sensation of physical pain, it also lessens the pain of rejection. I haven't tried it myself, but dozens of my friends and colleagues have and they all say the same thing: once it kicks in, access to their usual levels of equanimity suddenly reappear.

Why does this work so well? Acetaminophen, the active ingredient in Tylenol, works by inhibiting the synthesis of chemical messengers called prostaglandins. These help to transmit pain signals and induce fever, so when the body sustains an injury or an illness, it produces prostaglandins in response. Acetaminophen reduces the pain by helping to block this signaling. Because our brains fire in response to rejection the same way as actual physical pain, Tylenol works to inhibit the same signals, thus soothing the feelings of rejection. [8]

Even though acetaminophen can be a friendly hack, it is no replacement for doing the work. I would never suggest that any medication or substance can free you from ever feeling fear, nor would I recommend this as something to use frequently.

When it comes down to it, the work toward releasing fear is still yours.

FEAR & LETTING GO

I write and teach about how important it is to follow dreams, to fulfill your potential, and to lead a life of purpose. I have shared how necessary it is to have certainty in the Creator and the process of life, and not cling tightly to things of the physical world. I counsel that to move forward we have to be willing to let go of our pasts, and to stop re-reading the last chapter in order to write the next one.

The move from LA to New York forced me to put my money where my mouth is. When I finished packing the house in Los Angeles and put all our furniture on the moving truck, I was suddenly bombarded with fear. What if it's too hard? What if I'm unhappy? What if my family is unhappy? Why am I doing this? What if this is a mistake?

It didn't help that during the week I spent packing, my husband was already in New York with our three older children. And, all of this was happening right before Thanksgiving and Chanukah, which is a time when I typically bake, decorate, entertain, light the fireplace, and enjoy the warmth of home during the holidays. It was just me, baby Abigail, and an empty house, amid the deconstruction of my old life. Moving is the symbolic death of an old way of life as we make way for our next incarnation – a new chapter with unlimited potential that I looked forward to with great anticipation... and trepidation. New York has been an incredible part of our journey and continues to be. Fear was a signal that I was ready to grow and even as I write this, I am so grateful I accepted the invitation.

FEAR & RELATIONSHIPS

Relationships are one of our highest opportunities for spiritual growth. They offer us a very special kind of workshop in which to know ourselves and each other in incredibly profound ways. Because relationships require vulnerability to be successful, they also become instant mirrors for our unresolved fears. These unresolved fears usually present themselves in the form of narratives or stories we hold in our minds about who we are and what we deserve.

It is in our nature to tell stories and to love stories, but there is a dark side to storytelling. We can adopt stories that are negative and untrue. Too often, we are unaware that a negative story is circling on repeat in our minds and making decisions for us. It is necessary in relationships to be aware of this, because unbeknownst to you, your story can create a divide between you and your loved ones.

They can be based in falsehoods or they can be based in reality, in something we created or in something we take on from others. Either way, the story that plays over and over in your head affects your interactions and reactions to your spouse, your partner, your friends, and your family. We've all heard the phrases, "You're taking things out of context," or, "You're making a mountain out of a molehill." Small things become a big deal when they fit into our uniquely crafted narratives.

For example, let's say a husband cheats on his wife. Though this is painful, sadly it is not an unheard of transgression within marriage. They make the decision to work through it together and end up staying together. The wife eventually accepts what has happened and forgives him. They look to the future of their marriage and nurture it in a whole new way, and things are feeling okay. Until one evening. They attend a friend's dinner party, and at some point the wife turns around to see her husband having a friendly, polite conversation with another woman. It's not an important conversation and is, in every way, an innocuous social interaction, but what happens? She becomes enraged. Not because of anything that is actually happening. The reality is her husband is talking to a woman at a party. But, the movie in her head is telling her an entirely different story. This story sounds like this: he's speaking to another woman and he's going to stray, he's going to cheat again, and he is going to leave me. That is her perception of the situation and her emotional reaction is very real. However, she is only reacting to a negative, feared-based story inside her head.

Another example is a child who grows up in a home where his mother is an alcoholic. Fast-forward a decade or so; he meets a wonderful woman, gets married, but if his wife has the occasional glass of wine, he becomes controlling and demanding because he's afraid one glass of wine will lead to finishing the bottle and his wife will behave like his mother did when he was growing up. He too is reacting to the story in his head. His reaction is based purely on his past reality and is completely at odds with what is actually happening in his present.

It takes an awareness of these fear-based stories to begin to change them. Once we shed Light on these inauthentic stories and fears and we stop feeding them, they begin to dissolve. Healing your story is no different than changing perspectives or applying new actions. It is just another step, another tool we use to eradicate fear from our consciousness.

"Just as any meditation
should begin with the question
'What do I want?' a meditation
to overcome phobia should
begin with the question
'Why do I really have this fear?'
Just asking the question plants
the seed for the answer. But
what is hidden is not the
information itself. What is
hidden is the desire to request
the information. Dig it out
and you will begin to make
progress toward alleviating
the fear through the memory
of what caused it."

– Rav Berg

CHAPTER 13:
Seven Tools For Working Through Your Fears

"Life is when there is certainty. When there is no certainty, we are not living because we're always living in fear."
– Rav Berg

T he ultimate way to eradicate fear from your life is to have trust in the Creator and trust in your process. Now, that's a big ask. The tools laid out in this chapter are geared to help you get closer to attaining freedom from fear. Just as my journey with fear was a long process, beginning in my childhood, yours is a process, too.

Tool 1: Naming Your Fears

Look back at your lists of fears from Chapter Four. You named fears in different areas of your life and chose three on which to focus. You labeled them as either being healthy, illogical, or real. Below, write your three main fears again and see if there is any change. **Do you still agree with the way you categorized your fears in the beginning?**

1. _____

2. _____

3. _____

Now that you have acknowledged and better understand your three most prominent fears, it's time to build an action plan to eliminate them.

Of the three, choose the one you would like to tackle first and write it below:

I would like to eliminate my fear of

_____

_____

_____

Take a moment to journal how your life, relationships, or specific experiences would change if this fear was removed.

_____

_____

_____

_____

_____

Tool 2: Burning Your Fears

As we move through understanding and removing our fears, there is another potent tool that can help you release feelings of fear and negative thoughts as they arise.

16th century Kabbalist, Rav Isaac Luria has shared that if you have a negative thought that is bothering you, envision this verse: *esh tamid tukad al hamizbeach,* "The fire shall ever be burning on the altar." (Leviticus 6:13)

אֵשׁ תָּמִיד תּוּקַד עַל הַמִּזְבֵּחַ

It works like this:
- Bring the fearful or negative thought into your mind.
- Meditate on the verse, *esh tamid tukad al hamizbeach,* אֵשׁ תָּמִיד תּוּקַד עַל הַמִּזְבֵּחַ and you can either visualize a fire, or if you have the ability to safely create a real fire, you can do that, as well.
- Whether you build a fire or envision that fire, it is important to throw your thoughts in as many times as it takes until you feel it is truly erased from your consciousness. The truth is, no matter how much work we have been doing,

even if we are following and using all of the tools every day, no change will occur until a real shift in our consciousness is made.

Our ability to shift our consciousness is one of our greatest strengths.

As we work toward removing fear and negativity, we do the work of awakening greater and greater positive thoughts. This, in turn, creates more and more Light in our lives and openings for more blessings. It makes this particular tool of burning our negative thoughts a very powerful one. And it can be done almost anywhere, anytime.

Tool 3: Diminishing Your Fear

Remembering the consciousness, "Fear is not an option," can be, in and of itself, a powerful practice but there is an even more in-depth way to actualize this mantra. These steps are a way to put this into action.

1. When fear comes in ask, "Why is this coming to me?"
2. Let go and trust. Say to yourself, "Fear exists so I can connect even further to the Creator."
3. Shift your consciousness. Tell yourself, "Fear is not an option!"
4. Meditate on the Tetragrammaton, the four letter name of God. The *Yud Kay Vav Kay*.

The Tetragrammaton represents a very high level of revelation of the Light of the Creator and casting our eyes upon the letters connects us to the Light and protection of the Creator. Look at the letters and meditate on one fear you would like to overcome. This is one of the most powerful tools I have ever come across for eradicating fear. Any time you have doubt, worry, or fear, look at this name and your fear will begin to dissipate. It's especially useful in high panic situations.

I was traveling once with a good friend of mine and we were flying in a small plane. I wasn't aware my friend had a fear of flying, but I became quickly aware of it once we hit some turbulence. In a small plane, you feel every bump, so even though the turbulence wasn't terrible, it was noticeable. My friend's fear grew exponentially within minutes. She became hysterical, stricken with panic; she was screaming expletives and shouting, "Oh my God, I don't want to die!" First of all, ummm, nobody wants to die! Her hysteria was so overwhelming and intense it began affecting other passengers. When I saw this wasn't going to dissipate on its own, I began helping her to calm down.

I explained to her that her fear and panic were doing nothing to help the situation. I always carry a laminated card of the Tetragrammaton in my wallet and I offered it to her. Once her mind was focused on the letters and the sound of my voice, she began to relax until we landed. Was her fear gone forever? No. To eradicate this fear completely she needs to ask herself why she has the fear in the first place and what's keeping it alive and to consistently shift her consciousness.

Sometimes, we hold onto a fear because it serves us in some way. For instance, mortality comes to the forefront when someone is confronted with turbulence in a small aircraft. Having a fear of dying can be transformed into powerful, positive actions if we use it to take full advantage of every day, to be present with friends and family, and to live every day to the fullest.

Tool 4: Trim Tabs

Of all of the types of fear, illogical fears are the most detrimental to us because they impede our ability to live life fully and are responsible for our most debilitating experiences. Illogical fears are our phobias, the everyday things that render us paralyzed.

Small steps and changes have never been more imperative than in the case of eradicating fear. When action is taken in small steps it can lead to great change.

The trim tab was invented by philosopher and engineer, Buckminster Fuller, or Bucky, as his friends knew him. For those of us who are nautically and aeronautically challenged, trim tabs are the tiny rudders attached to the back of the larger rudders on either ships or aiplanes, and they offer assistance to the main rudder by mitigating pressure.

Bucky understood that if such large vessels change direction too quickly, the sheer force alone would put too much pressure on the main rudder, causing it to snap. So, he devised a solution where that kind of pressure was eliminated, and thus, the trim tab was born. Fuller explained, "Just moving the little trim tab builds a low pressure that pulls that rudder around. It takes almost no effort at all. So you can just put your foot out and the whole big ship is going to move." What he meant was, the seemingly tiny amount of change the trim tab offered made a dramatic difference in the direction of the ship. You can test this yourself the next time you are on a raft in the pool, or in a canoe or rowboat. Simply dangle your hand in the water off one side of the back of the craft and the whole thing will gently turn in that direction. [9]

This concept reminds me of a quote I read in one of Nancy Gibbs' articles, "It's funny how things change slowly until the day we realize that they've changed completely." This is true of your fear. By taking small steps and making small changes, one day you will wake up and the fear will be no more.

Your trim tabs can be any small changes you can make to align yourself with certainty and effectively steer yourself away from fear.

In what ways can you make small, immediate changes to your current reality that can help you to eliminate fear? If you're tackling a phobia such as flying and you have an upcoming flight, download a few meditations and practice them beforehand. By doing this, you're creating a space in your mind you can easily access when fear arises, and from that place of calm, you can assure yourself and reconnect to certainty.

Make a list of trim tabs below:

_____

_____

_____

_____

Tool 5: Make Your Anti-Fear Mantra

Another useful tool for eradicating fear-based thoughts is turning your fear around and making it into an affirmative mantra. This is an opportunity to remove the fear and connect back to the Light. Let's use the example of someone who is fearful of public speaking.

The fearful thought is:
I'm unprepared. I feel like a fraud. I'll be visibly shaken, I'll forget what I want to say, and no one will ever want to hear me speak again. I'll be humiliated.

The mantra is:

I am fully prepared. Everything I have to say is helpful, well-founded, and something I believe in. I will appear cool, calm, and collected.

By simply reversing your fear, you have created a mantra that not only empowers you but also eliminates the fearful origin. Practice turning a few of your own fearful thoughts into empowering mantras.

The thought is:

_____

The mantra is:

_____

The thought is:

_____

The mantra is:

_____

Tool 6: Engage Your Body

Amy Cuddy is a social psychologist and a Harvard Business School Professor who gave a TED Talk that illustrated the idea and psychology behind "power poses". In a "power pose" a person is relaxed and open, their shoulders are square, spine is straight, chest is lifted, and hands are on hips. Cuddy researched whether or not different poses affected people physically and mentally. Participants assuming power poses were more tolerant to risk and saw 20% spikes in testosterone, the dominance hormone. The overall result: strike a powerful pose, feel more powerful.[10]

This is a simple practice that can be done anywhere. Find a quiet area where you can be alone and strike a powerful pose! Physically embody Superman or Wonder Woman or anyone who invokes a sense of fearlessness in you. Engaging your body in this way not only takes your mind off of your fear, it gets you into the physical and mental modes of confidence, strength, and power.

Tool 7: Time Travel

The kabbalists teach there is a name of God written in Hebrew that is a channel for certainty and removal of fear. It can be used any time, around any fear, and works like a fear eraser. By simply looking at and focusing on this name we can go back to a place before we had the fear. This name is a conduit of Light and is not meant to be said aloud - אכדט״ם.

Each Hebrew name is a channel for a different energy. Elokim (אלהים) is the name that is a conduit for the energy of judgment and negativity. This means that when we are experiencing something that is causing us fear, we are actually connected to the energy of the name Elokim (אלהים).

Now, the name אכדט״ם is created by using the preceding letters in the Hebrew alphabet with the letters in the name Elokim (אלהים) which energetically means we are connecting to a time before the fear.

Let's break this down in English. The word that connects to doubt is FEAR. Ergo, we replace the letters F E A R with the letters that immediately precede it in the alphabet, giving us EDAQ. English letters are not channels for energy, however, Hebrew letters are.

By meditating on אכדט״ם, we are actually connecting ourselves to the energy that existed before the fear we are currently experiencing.

Just as FEAR became EDAQ, Elokim (אלהים) becomes אכדט״ם in the following manner:

- א has no preceding letter, so it remains the same: א
- ל is changed to the letter כ
- ה becomes ד
- י becomes ט
- ם remains ם, because the letter before Final Mem is Regular Mem, but by being at the end of the name it turns to Final Mem.

Any time you feel yourself experiencing negativity or fear use this tool. You were not born with this fear, so there was a time in your life before the fear existed. This meditation works like time travel, taking you back to the natural peace and calm you had before you acquired this fear – to the fearless place of your true being.

CHAPTER 14:

Make an Action Plan

N ow that you have the consciousness and the tools, it's time to put them into action. We are going to use examples of illogical fears to illustrate these plans, but they can be just as easily applied to any fear-based thought. After we have identified our fear, it's time to challenge our fearful thoughts. Remember to incorporate the consciousness and tools above into your custom plan to help you eradicate fear from your life experience.

THREE STEPS FOR ERADICATING FEAR

Step 1: Plan for the Morning

"The world is new to us every morning – this is God's gift; and every man should believe he is reborn each day."
– Baal Shem Tov

Roy Baumeister, a renowned psychologist and self-control researcher, states that our willpower is a finite resource. We only have so much stamina in the day with which to tackle the big decisions and changes we want to make. This means we need to be smart about how we use our willpower. It has been scientifically proven that our willpower and psychological stamina are at their strongest in the morning, waning throughout the day. This is why, for anyone who has ever dieted, it is so easy to choose a smoothie for breakfast and a salad for lunch, and then make an unhealthy choice around dinner time. It is simply because we have exhausted our willpower by day's end. Knowing this, we can plan for optimum levels of success by planning the tough stuff – like facing our fears – for the earlier part of the day.[11]

I know a woman who is terrified of driving on freeways. She lives in Southern California, and if you have ever visited this area you know freeways are an essential element of transportation. Because her willpower will be strongest in the earlier part of the day, it is a perfect time for her to practice by driving from one exit to another on the freeway.

To put it simply, if you can, face your fears in the morning, not at night. Make a plan to apply these steps in the morning, and not in the evening when your energy and willpower take a natural dip.

Step 2: Challenge Fear-Based Thoughts

Let's use the example of a fear of flying. The thoughts that arise around this fear are usually overly negative and statistically unlikely. As you sit in the terminal waiting for your flight, watching planes land and take off, you may begin to feel your chest tighten or your breath quicken. You imagine what it would feel like to be 33,000 feet in the air when turbulence begins and you begin to panic. In this moment, instead of focusing on your physical response to fear, notice your thoughts.

They will likely fall into one of three categories:

1. Prophesying
During this type of thought process you tell yourself exactly how you will feel and exactly what will happen. An example would be saying to yourself, "I'm going to get onto the plane and mid-flight I'm going have a panic attack."

2. Overgeneralizing
Overgeneralizing says, "Because something happened one time, it will happen every time." For example, "The last time I flew on an airplane, I had a panic attack, so I'm never flying again."

3. Catastrophizing
This one is the most common. This is a thought process that jumps you to the most extreme outcome with little or no evidence to support that it is even possible, never mind probable. An example of a catastrophizing thought would be, "I'm going to get on the plane; it's going to crash." Again, there is no evidence whatsoever supporting that your plane will crash and, in fact, all statistical evidence points to the contrary.

Because I have experienced an elevator phobia, we'll use my catastrophizing thoughts to look at how we can challenge fearful thinking in the moment.

My most elaborate version of this fear would be "I'll get stuck in an elevator on the 48th floor where there's no cell reception, my anxiety will cause my mouth to dry (which is a physiological fear response), I'll be stuck for hours without any water, the air will be thick, I won't be able to breathe, and it's a long holiday weekend, so chances are I won't be found until Tuesday and now, the lights just went out..."

In the moment you can ask yourself the following questions:

Q: What around me currently contradicts this thought?

"It's Wednesday, it's not a holiday weekend. The elevator seems new and is running smoothly. I have a bottle of water in my bag."

Q: Is there an action you could take if this situation were to occur?

"I could always call for assistance using the elevator's own alarm and there is no indication that my cell phone won't work. There are also people who love me and would notice if I was gone for very long."

Q: Is this thought fear-based?

"Yes, I can clearly see that I am catastrophizing. There is no evidence that what I fear will come true and all evidence is to the contrary."

Challenging your thoughts in this way gets to the root of the fear and cuts off its life force. If your fear-based thoughts have nowhere to grow, eventually they will disintegrate.

Step 3: Exposure

In order to overcome your fears, you must expose yourself to them, which I recommend doing in small doses. Taking on too much too quickly can result in an overwhelming, and therefore detrimental, experience that can compound your fears. Just like trim tabs, it's the small changes that make the biggest difference. It's like running up a hill: you need to go one step at a time. This is exactly how exposure works. You are standing in your fear at the bottom of the hill, and at the top is your life without that fear. The hill is exposure. Let's look at this through the lens of someone with the fear of being outside their home.

The steps can look like this:

Step 1: Spend time looking outside through an open window.

Step 2: Open your front door and stand outside on your porch.

Step 3: Go outside and walk to the sidewalk.

Step 4: Go outside, walk to the sidewalk, then walk to the front of your neighbor's house.

Step 5: Go outside and walk to the corner of your block.

Step 6: Walk around your block.

Working with fear in this new way takes time to get used to, like exercising a muscle for the very first time. You don't need to change your life overnight but you can begin to release fear slowly by taking baby steps. This is exactly what the hill exercise does.

I am reminded of a time shortly after Josh and Miriam were born, a time when my adrenal glands were still not quite functioning at their best. My family and I thought it would be fun to spend the day together at an amusement park. I used to love roller coasters and thrill rides. Michael doesn't really love heights, but I convinced everyone it would be fun to go on this huge roller coaster, not realizing how things that used to thrill me were now absolutely terrifying. So, there we were inching up the slope, the track clicking slowly to the top, and the anticipation growing. Surprisingly, I found myself feeling increasingly uncomfortable. As we crept higher and higher upwards to the top, a sense of panic arose in me.

As we arrived at the first peak of the coaster (there were many more to come), there was a little mechanical bear waving happily. I'm sure he was designed to be adorable, yet all I could think was how he was symbolic of something dreadful that was about to occur and this was the last happy image I would ever have. Why else would they put this adorable bear at the most terrifying part of this terrifying ride? At this point my heart was pounding, my breathing tight and short, and I felt like I was having a heart attack. I actually considered jumping off onto the platform next to the bear. Eventually someone would come get me down. This was an actual thought I had, a plan that I had devised in my mind that seemed to me completely normal and plausible. Logic did chime in for a moment. I imagined the embarrassment of my husband and children as I would appear on the evening news as the deranged woman that jumped off of a roller coaster.

Fortunately, the reality of that thought also set in. I saw how incredibly not normal that was and stopped myself from entertaining this thought any further. In fact, I became more frightened of the thought than the roller coaster. I told myself how crazy my escape plan was and that I was not going to be that person. So, I closed my eyes and focused my mind on a happier place until the ride ended.

I noticed this fear, and before allowing it to grow, I worked through it using exposure. I went on every single roller coaster in the entire park that day. For I knew if I didn't, I would have left the park that day with roller coasters having become a new fear and as we know now, fear that goes unchecked becomes a planted seed that roots itself and grows. By choosing exposure in the moment, I stopped the growth and eliminated the fear.

Tackling our fear in small steps not only helps to eradicate it slowly and surely, it also nurtures our confidence.

The exposure hill can be applied to any fear and is guaranteed to work if you continue applying it. Think of a fear you have currently and start to trek your own hill. As fears arise, challenge the thoughts that arise with them. Ask yourself in every moment,

What am I choosing?

Is it comfort over curiosity?

Am I choosing my limiting beliefs?

Or am I choosing to grow and expand?

Ask yourself these questions daily and always remember that fear is not an option.

Step 4: Create Your Exposure Hill

Now it's time to cement our changed perspective by building an exposure hill. Take your fear and beginning with the smallest step, create your exposure hill. Start with six steps:

Step 1: _____

Step 2: _____

Step 3: _____

Step 4: _____

Step 5: _____

Step 6: _____

As you accomplish each new step, acknowledge your progress. Take a minute to feel proud of your growth. Scientifically, adults respond to rewards in the same way that children do. So, as you make accomplishments, set up a reward system for yourself in order to create a positive feedback loop. It will keep you motivated to continue pushing through the fear. Then, once you complete the first six steps, choose six more that build upon your progress.

As you work through your action plan, if at any point you feel overwhelmed, panicked, or anxious, take a step back. Turn your awareness within and look to your immediate thoughts. Remind yourself again that fear is not an option.

While writing this book, I was on a ski trip in Vermont. I liked the idea of skiing but, having lived in LA for so long, I hadn't been on skis for a long time. Now that we are living in a snowy climate I have more opportunities to practice but I am always starting as a beginner and that comes with anxiety.

After a day of getting reacquainted with my skis, I decided to try a new mountain that required an intermediate skill level. As I rode the lift up with my instructor, I began to feel anxious. He explained there were steep areas I needed to watch for. Of course, he told me this while we were already on the lift, which only compounded my nervousness. But, as I stood at the top of the slope, I knew I had to choose, either certainty or anxiety. Because the two cannot co-exist.

As I was gliding down the mountain I began speaking to myself, "Fear is not an option! You are one with the Creator! Monica, you've got this!" I repeated it out loud, over and over, and sure enough my fear eventually gave way to excitement and exhilaration. I even approached the steep section and, without any panic, decided to side step down, breaking back into my usual stride when it felt right. It was a blast!

When I reached the bottom my instructor congratulated me on the run. "Let's do it again!" I exclaimed.

He was taken aback. He expressed that all the students who had skied that slope for the first time never wanted a repeat. The steep section startled them so terribly they didn't opt to do a second time. But I knew if I didn't it would escalate into a new fear. So, I did the run again, this time taking on the steep section and it was a success.

We don't necessarily lose more fears as we mature, in fact, we seem to be inclined to new fears unless we are conscious and make a real effort to dispel them as they surface. Had I let this tiny bit of fear and discomfort decide for me, I would have missed out on a beautiful experience.

CHAPTER 15:

Seven Things I Want My Daughters To Know To Become Fearless Women

I dedicate this chapter to my daughters, Miriam and Abigail. They have taught me so much about what it means to be fearless and my wish for them is to know their own fearlessness, and live their lives to the fullest... May you pass this on to the women you love.

1. Your Body Is Part of Your Expression

You are physically strong. Use your body, your strong legs, your graceful hands, your sassy hips. Remain fearless in your body and don't ever allow yourself to hate any part. Your body is perfect and strong.

2. Never Be Ashamed of Your Passions

Follow your bliss. Do what speaks to you, read about what interests you, be friends with the people you like, and don't let others' opinions about what you love embarrass you. Never give up on who you are or what you believe in for someone else. You are 100% worthwhile and whole, just as you are.

3. Make Friends

As Epicurus stated, "Of all the things that wisdom provides for living one's entire life in happiness, the greatest by far, is the possession of friendship." Always be open to making new friends. Old friends who are true are not going to be alienated by new friends. Not every friend will stay in your life forever, and that's okay. Some friends come to us at particular times of life and then go when that time period is over. While it hurts to lose a friend, it should never keep you from being open and sharing yourself with new people. Remember, everyone in your life started out as a stranger.

4. Talk to Me – Even If We Disagree

You can always tell me what you are feeling or thinking, even if you know I will disagree. It's okay to disagree with me. I want you to feel safe to express any emotion, and share any scenario with me. Know that I love you unconditionally and there is nothing you could ever do or say that will make me stop loving you. You have a unique voice and I always want to hear it. I learn from you all the time and I don't want to miss any of the lessons you have to teach me.

5. You Are Beautiful

I know I'm your mom and you sense bias, but it's the truth. In your face I see the baby you were, the beautiful girl you are today, and the woman you will one day become. Know your worth and your value. Don't waste years of your life trying to convince yourself that you are beautiful and powerful and special. You are. Don't waste your time feeling less-than. You are more than enough and you will accomplish great things.

6. You Are Your Own Person

You and I have many things in common, but you aren't me. You are not destined to live the life I have or experience the same challenges. Your path is your own and I want very much to help guide you where your unique spirit needs to take you.

7. It's Them, Not You

Nearly every time someone hurts you, lashes out, or says something that makes you feel insecure or unworthy, it's a manifestation of their own pain. It has very little to do with you, other than you happened to be in their proximity. Everyone is fighting their own battles and conflicts will arise. People will be hurtful or nasty and yes, it will hurt. Just remember, it's really not about you, it's about them. While you can learn something from the experience you do not need to accept their judgments as facts.

Epilogue

An affirmation to replace fear with
certainty, trust, and love.

I am **FULLY CAPABLE** of handling any
challenges that arise in my day and my life.
I **TRUST EVERYTHING** that happens to me is
for my greatest good.
FEAR IS NOT AN OPTION.
I have total and complete **TRUST** in the Creator.
I choose to connect to the **LIGHT** in
every situation.
FEAR IS NOT AN OPTION.
I meet every event and circumstance with the
CERTAINTY it will work out for the best.
I am whole and **COMPLETE.**
FEAR IS NOT AN OPTION.
I can achieve my greatest goals and **DREAMS.**
I am living in and as my **TRUEST SELF.**

FEAR IS NOT AN OPTION.

Acknowledgments

I dedicate this book to my teachers, my mentors, and completely by the grace of God, my parents-in-law, Rav and Karen Berg. From the time you entered my life it has never been the same.

Rav, you taught me, more accurately yelled at me, with loving strength one fateful night that "Fear Is Not an Option." Thank you for walking me through, not around, the most difficult experiences of my life. You have made the most profound impact on me and helped to pave my life's work.

Karen, thank you for teaching me how to live fearlessly, and to never be afraid to speak up about what I believe in or to go after my dreams. You, more than anyone, have taught me that if I want something I need to make it happen and, to do so, fear must be removed from my lexicon.

Some of the chapters in this book are named after my immediate family. Michael, you may have noticed that there isn't a chapter named after you. This is because you have never been a source of fear for me. In fact, whenever I have come face-to-face with my deepest fears you are the one who stands beside me hand-in-hand, prepared to face any challenge head on with me. You always show up.

In life, with everything we've faced, both great and small, having you as my best friend, lover, and life partner has been my greatest source of strength. Your love creates an environment for me to thrive and flourish.

To my children, David, Joshua, Miriam, and Abigail, may you always live your lives being courageous, certain, and kind. I know I cannot protect you from your life experiences, but I hope I can give you the tools to protect, heal, and be yourselves... your best selves. (Thank you for letting me be your mamma.)

Liz, after all the words we have shared and interchanged, I seem to be at a loss as how to adequately express my appreciation and gratitude for all you do and all you are to me. One of my favorite quotes that Gwyeth Paltrow said is, "Our friends can become our historians, secret-keepers, and partners in life's journey." We started out having a strictly work relationship, and somewhere along the line you became my cherished friend and the voice of reason in my head when it all just seems too hard.

Dearest Annie, it's surreal to me that you won't be able to read this book, as you always encouraged me to be authentic and to never be afraid to be seen. I feel you watching me from above. Thank you for encouraging me to trust my intuition and not doubt myself; this was your biggest gift to me. As you always said, "Truth is Truth." It certainly is... This quote from Steve Jobs always reminds me of your sage advice, "Don't let the noise of others' opinions drown out your own inner voice. And most importantly, have the courage to follow your heart and intuition... Everything else is secondary." I love you and miss you, Annie.

I have always been a firm believer that you need to give attention to all aspects of you... body, mind and spirit. To my dear friend Tracy, I can't recount how many times over the last decade, I have walked into your studio working through an emotion, or searching for an answer to a problem only to walk out two hours later, with clarity and feeling empowered. Thank you for teaching me how to use my body in a way that gives me strength instead of the way I used to use it, depleting it and running it down. More than anything, thank you for being a trusted friend and confidant, it's meant more to me than you know.

Mom, Dad, Rebecca, and Jessica, we are fortunate to share so much love among us. We are a family that simply supports each other's dreams and promotes happiness in one another. Thank you for always loving me.

Mama Nouran, you are courageous and an amazing example of strength for me. All of the heartache you've experienced in your life has only made your capacity to love greater. I am fortunate to have been on the receiving end of your continuous and unconditional love. You are the ultimate matriarch.

I believe the Creator sends us help exactly when we need it. Kelly, thank you for your hard work, and your rare and infectious smile that greeted me even when I offered you a difficult task.

I also feel compelled to thank Reut who, after attending a lecture I gave on fear, said to me, "You must write a book about this. People need to hear this." Thank you for the repeated suggestions.

To the opposition, thank you very much. And to all of those who are struggling with their own opposers remember:

"Keep away from people who try to belittle your ambitions. Small people always do that, but really great ones make you feel that you could become great."
 – Mark Twain

Medical Disclaimer

This book is not intended as a substitute for the medical advice of physicians. The reader should regularly consult a physician in matters relating to his/her health and particularly with respect to any symptoms that may require diagnosis or medical attention.

References

[1] Latané, Bibb, and John M. Darley. "Group Inhibition of Bystander Intervention in Emergencies." Journal of Personality and Social Psychology. 10.3. (1968): 215-221. American International School of Guangzhou. Web. Apr. 2017.

[2] Eddy, Cheryl. "5 Crime Victims Who Survived and Helped Nail Their Attackers." Gizmodo. Gizmodo Media Group, 30 Oct. 2015. Web. Nov. 2016.

[3] Berg, Rav. "Prayer," Living Wisdom. Kabbalah Centre International. October 22, 2014. Web. May 11, 2017.

[4] Dweck, Carol. Mindset. Carol Dweck. 2010. Web. Nov. 2016.

[5] Popova, Maria. "Fixed vs. Growth: The Two Basic Mindsets That Shape Our Lives." BrainPickings. BrainPickings.org, 29 Jan. 2014. Web. Nov. 2016.

[6] Rascal Flatts. "God Bless The Broken Road" Lyric. Street Records, 2004. CD.

[7] Estrada, Chris. "Plushenko to the critics: 'Thank you very much.'" NBC Sports. NBC Universal. 9 Feb. 2014. Web. Jan 2017.

[8] Stix, Gary. "Feeling the Pain of Rejection? Try Taking a Tylenol." Scientific American. Nature America, Inc. 1 Sep. 2010. Web. Nov 2016.

[9] Popova, Maria. "Buckminster Fuller's Brilliant Metaphor for the Greatest Key to Transformation and Growth." BrainPickings. BrainPickings.org, 21 Aug. 2015. Web. Nov. 2016.

[10] Cuddy, Amy. "Your Body Language Shapes Who You Are." TED: Ideas Worth Spreading. Ted Conf., Jun. 2012. Web. Nov. 2016.

[11] Vanderkam, Laura. "Can You Learn Willpower?" CBS News. CBS Interactive Inc. 22 Sep. 2011. Web. Apr. 2017.